T0146615

FUEL

FUEL

WHAT IT TAKES TO SURVIVE AS AN ENTREPRENEUR

JOSH YORK

FUEL
WHAT IT TAKES TO SURVIVE AS AN ENTREPRENEUR

iUniverse books may be ordered through booksellers or by contacting:

iUniverse
1663 Liberty Drive
Bloomington, IN 47403
www.iuniverse.com
1-800-Authors (1-800-288-4677)

ISBN: 978-1-5320-3719-1 (sc)
ISBN: 978-1-5320-3717-7 (hc)
ISBN: 978-1-5320-3718-4 (e)

Library of Congress Control Number: 2018901577

Print information available on the last page.

iUniverse rev. date: 03/01/2018

CONTENTS

Dedication vii

Acknowledgments ix

Chapter 1 Who We Are and Who I Am 1

Chapter 2 A Misspent Youth? 11

Chapter 3 Who Wants to Work for a Boss? 17

Chapter 4 The Vision 27

Chapter 5 Execution 39

Chapter 6 The Struggle 49

Chapter 7 Work Is Not a Dirty Word 61

Chapter 8 Fuel 69

Chapter 9 Drive 81

Chapter 10 Balance 91

DEDICATION

To the entire GYMGUYZ family. Your passion and energy is the FUEL our brand uses to continue changing people's lives.

ACKNOWLEDGMENTS

I don't even know where to start…..There are so many people who believed in the vision. To my parents for their love and support for letting me use their dining room as the first GYMGUYZ office. To the entire corporate team. Thank you for your talent, passion and dedication. It is so gratifying to have so much love for each and every one of you.

To our franchise family members. You all continue to DRIVE and FUEL your businesses with passion and I can't thank you enough. The amount of respect and appreciation I have for you is indescribable.

I want to thank our vendors for believing in my vision from the beginning. You guyz have been with us through thick and thin and I want to let you know how much I appreciate that.

Finally, to my incredible and amazing wife Stacy and son Jake. I love you guyz so much and appreciate all the love and support you have given me on this crazy roller coaster ride to the top. Unless you're an entrepreneur, no one understands the challenges and sacrifices that must be made. I wrote this book because I wanted to share my insights and show you how you can turn a vision into a reality! I look forward to writing more books in the future.

WHO WE ARE AND WHO I AM

In school, we're all taught to solve problems—math problems, multiple-choice tests, true and false. For the most part, the problems are all on paper. Then when we graduate school, we discover that we can carry phones in our pockets that make math problems irrelevant. We realize, only a few people care about grammar and that the problems on paper aren't the real problems. Basically, nothing is like it was on our school tests. Now we've got to deal with stained clothing when we have job interviews, figure out when to see our friends, try to plan dates but can't, because we need to work overtime to pay mortgages. We've got to solve the problem of getting to work even though the car's broken down— or how we're going to make time to attend a wedding. And on top of all that, we've got to get to the gym for some exercise.

While school was interesting, it wasn't where I wanted to be. I was eager to get started, even when I wasn't sure exactly what my career was going to be. I just couldn't wait. All I knew for certain was that I wanted to change people's lives for the better. When I finally finished school with my bachelor's degree (which wasn't too long ago), I had to figure out what I wanted to do with my life. This was a new problem for me since school had always given me a purpose. It was something to do, and it took up a lot of time. Even then there wasn't enough time in the day to get in my workout. And eventually I realized that everybody has that same problem, well into adulthood. With jobs, kids, and social lives, fitting in an hour for exercise is never just an hour. It's childcare and changing in the locker room and the commute to and from the gym. It's squeezing in phone calls while you're driving and having to rush through a shower just to make it home for dinner.

After school, as I was working in a job that wasn't right for me, I fell back on my ability to solve problems. That was the one thing I was always good at: observing a situation and finding out a way to improve it. Knowing that my job wasn't providing me with the life I wanted to live and seeing how hard it is for pretty much everybody to fit everything he or she wants and needs to do in his or her daily schedule, I realized that I could solve two problems at once. I could give my life a purpose and help people manage their time to get in that all-important exercise.

I'm Josh York, and you're about to read my story. It's a story about finding your place in the world and how the world will reward your efforts. I want to share my story because I think it will provide you with a rousing example of overcoming obstacles, struggling to realize dreams, and making a system that works. I'm the founder and CEO of GYMGUYZ. My business is revolutionizing the fitness industry by being the first in-home mobile personal training franchise. So, what do we do? We come to the setting of your choice to lead you through a convenient, customized, and creative workout. Those are our three Cs. Think of us as an on-demand personal training service. We can train you anywhere, from your home, office, pool, park, place of worship, hospital, senior home, and so on. We've done workouts in parking lots, and we've done workouts in supermarkets. And we love changing lives.

Instead of our clients traveling to a gym to get in their workouts, we bring expertise and motivation right into their homes.

So many people doubted me and told me it was impossible, but I didn't listen to a word they had to say. I never gave up. I was persistent. I saw a problem, and I solved it.

My story starts before I even thought of GYMGUYZ. I began building a family by searching for mentors. I knew I wanted to be successful, and to do that, I found other people who were successful and learned everything I could from them. Among them are seven people who run billion-dollar companies. If you surround yourself with great people, great things will happen.

I like to think of GYMGUYZ as a family whose members work together toward one goal: changing people's lives for the better. If you have a gym membership, you have to go to the gym to take advantage of it. We at GYMGUYZ make it possible to forego all that extra time by coming directly to you with a van packed full of equipment to customize your exercise to fit your needs. We have 365 pieces of training equipment, from kettlebells to kickboxing equipment to weights, one for every day of the year. We began in New York, but we've expanded through franchising to bring our services throughout the United States and beyond.

We begin our role in a client's life with a free assessment, which looks at the client in terms of numbers in relation to body, nutrition, and fitness. We then design a routine to help develop a lifestyle that encourages health and well-being.

The best way to understand a GYMGUYZ exercise routine is to go back to our three Cs: convenient, customized, and creative. What's more convenient than our bringing the gym to you? Through our assessment and expertise, we customize your workout to suit your needs. And that workout is going to be creative in how it approaches fitness and a healthy lifestyle. We don't want you to see exercise as a chore. We want you to love doing it.

On one of the bright red walls in my office hangs a photograph of Secretariat and Ron Turcotte racing at Belmont Stakes to win the Triple Crown. As Secretariat gallops ahead of the pack, Turcotte, who regularly rode the famous horse, is glancing back over his left shoulder. The nearest horse is thirty-one lengths behind them. It's not hard to imagine what Turcotte is thinking: *They'll never catch us.*

During that race in 1973, Secretariat set a record for the mile-and-a-half race on dirt that has yet to be broken. The most recent winner, in 2017, was a full six seconds slower. It's an outstanding achievement, and because of it, Secretariat might be the only racehorse that the American public knows by name. That race itself is an interesting story. Secretariat was even with another horse for the first half, only pulling away because his stamina enabled him to keep up his speed while the others tired. A lot of jockeys, when seeing that they have such an insurmountable lead, would pull back a little, telling the horse to slow down just coast to the finish. Not Turcotte. He knew what was possible for that horse on that day, so Secretariat was allowed to do what he did best.

Turcotte understood that they weren't just winning a race— they were accomplishing something no one had done before. Years of training, expertise, and drive had led them to that moment.

I first saw that photo, taken by Bob Coglianese in the office of one of our franchise family members. I loved it immediately, and that family member's father was gracious enough to give me a framed print of it as a gift. That made me love it even more because it lends the image greater personal significance; now I look at it and think about how much GYMGUYZ meant to that father because of the role it played in his family's life. Since then, Secretariat (who was also called Big Red) has become my model for GYMGUYZ. That horse, in that moment, embodies two of the most important ideas behind GYMGUYZ: scalability and FUEL.

Scalability is your business concept's capacity for growth. A business is scalable if it can work on large and small scales without major modification. I envisioned GYMGUYZ to be scalable from the start. FUEL describes the core components that can make any enterprise a success: fun, unity, earnings, and leadership. The components are goals, but they're also motivation. We'll explore these concepts in greater depth in later chapters.

Throughout this book, I demonstrate the way I've thought about the elements of entrepreneurship and how I execute my ideas. No business succeeds based solely on improvisation. You can't make it up as you go along. You've got to think through every aspect of your business model. For example, the GUYZ part of GYMGUYZ means something specific: genuine, unique, you can do it, and zero excuses. That's our business model in a nutshell. We're genuine because we can deliver what we promise. We're unique; nobody else does what we do. And yes, you can do it. We know that regular exercise is tough for so many different reasons. We cut through all those reasons to help with, again, convenience, but we also motivate you to succeed. We're there for you, and that gives you zero excuses.

You might have seen our vans driving down the road, on the way to conduct an exercise session. Our vans are bright red, and that's not random. Red represents power, strength, passion, determination, and desire. It's energizing. It excites the emotions and motivates you to take action. We sweat red, day in and day out, and we will sweat red worldwide. We started in New

York and moved across the United States, even into Hawaii. We expanded into Canada in 2017, and that's just the beginning.

So how did all this become possible? It's a combination of factors, just like everything else in business. This book is an exercise in describing and exploring those factors, which I think can be valuable for anyone interested in pursuing the entrepreneurial life.

When it comes down to it, there are recurring themes, traits, and ideas that are vital to succeeding as an entrepreneur. First and foremost, I've never chased after the money. I chase the vision (we'll get into the vision in chapter 4). Part of that vision has always been helping people and changing the world. I never lose track of that.

Second, I think of the people who work with me as a family, not as employees. I want you to reconsider the whole idea of being a boss. I think a lot of people dread going to work every day because they don't work in an environment that allows them to feel comfortable. The hierarchy becomes more important than the work being accomplished and that leads to dissatisfied employees. You are going to spend hours and hours with the people who work for you, so make sure that it's time everyone can say is worthwhile.

Finally, you've got to be willing to execute no matter what obstacles stand in your way. You've got to be able to realize your vision, sacrificing when necessary, doing what needs to be done to succeed. To get what I want out of life, to live the way that I want to live, I've got to be true to myself. I'm a freakin' beast because that's what I have to be. I get up before four o'clock every day, when it's dark and quiet. That's the place to start. Every day is an opportunity to grow, expand, and make yourself and your family better. It's true for exercise, and it's true for business. Without the hard work—which requires patience, thought, and determination—you won't succeed.

The rest of the book flows from those concepts. Chapter 2 gives a little bit of an autobiography, up until I finished college, for context, and in part, to demonstrate that succeeding as an entrepreneur is possible from any starting point. I like to think that I'm not your average person, but that doesn't mean what I've done is impossible for everybody else. You might have noticed that those three traits I described above—constructing a vision instead of chasing money, thinking of the people I work with as a family, and the willingness to execute—aren't skills that it takes years to acquire. To some extent, they require discipline, but everyone reading this can achieve them.

Chapter 3 is about what happened after college. It was a tough time, since I got a job that wasn't right for me. But I got through it and in the process learned a lot of lessons about how I wanted to live and what I wanted out of life. It's the time when I first started painting my vision, and a lot of the inspiration came because I was in a situation that really depressed me. I knew I had to do *something* to change my situation, and in figuring out how to solve that problem, I started GYMGUYZ.

Chapter 4 gives you the details about my vision for GYMGUYZ, along with advice on how to paint your own. I lean heavily on painting as a metaphor for this process, which I think is useful for conceptualizing a career and communicating it to other people.

Chapter 5 is all about execution. I had the vision but no money. How could I succeed? You'll find out. Chapter 6 is about the struggle to build a worldwide brand. It's a long process, and so it continues into chapter 7, which shows you the grind. These are stories about the obstacles, difficulties, and unexpected troubles that pop up in building a business. In the end, success is only possible because of persistence.

I like to make my ideas memorable, so I've worked out some acronyms: FUEL and DRIVE. These come into play in the later chapters of this book. Chapter 8 is about seeing the light at the end of the tunnel and finding the fuel to get you there— that's where we'll explore what FUEL is all about: fun, unity, earnings, and leadership. It's where the dreams start to come true. Chapter 9 is all about DRIVE: determination, respect, integrity, versatility, and excellence. You've got to work hard to be the best, all day every day; but that hard work pays off if you can put together the different necessary components. That's what DRIVE demonstrates. And chapter 10 closes things up by giving insight into how I roll. It's the balance between work and life that makes achieving the dream possible.

2

A MISSPENT YOUTH?

It took me a long time to figure out what I wanted to be when I grew up. At first, I wanted to be a hockey player. I came home from school every day, threw down my backpack, and got out my hockey gear. Ice time can be hard to come by in New York, but my friends and I managed. I might have been able to make it on a professional team if I'd stuck with it, but by the time I was a teenager, my priorities and perspective had changed. I became aware of the realities of being a professional athlete. The time spent on the road didn't appeal to me anymore. I wanted to stay in one place most of the time, closer to family and friends.

I was especially close with my brother Jason, who has been a huge help in my life and career. Our family wasn't especially wealthy, so I had a lot of different jobs. I worked in a coffee shop, in an appliance center, in restaurants, delivering newspapers and flyers, doing clerical work, in a doctor's office, and more. I didn't last long in any of these jobs. I would keep a job for a few days before quitting because I wasn't passionate about the work. The one thing I have been passionate about for a long time is fitness.

Even back as far as high school, I felt the need to work out every day, and I was trying to make that need fit in the rest of my schedule. I was figuring out how; the only problem was that nobody else saw it that way. I was frustrated by the fact that school took up time that I could have used to work out. You can see that my mind was already on track toward today—toward GYMGUYZ.

I think the reason I didn't thrive in school comes down to the process. Sitting in a room, listening to someone talk all the time—this isn't a process for me. I prefer the process of business, which feels more natural because it involves dealing with problems that arise as you accomplish your goals. But there was one thing about school that I liked, and that was the resources. See, workouts were my thing, and I knew that even as a teenager. They made me feel whole. There's something about setting your whole body to a task, when you've got your mind focused on it, that makes it unlike the drudgery of other things. When you're sitting in class, your body is essentially doing nothing. That's why it's so easy to get distracted. At school we had access to the gym, to teachers, and to friends. You can't overestimate the importance of access to the right resources.

I also learned important lessons in school, of course. I don't think you can get through high school without learning that showing up every day does have its benefits. That might be the origin of my persistence and patience: having to simply get through it, going to school every day and waiting for years for the payoff. We're all given a goal when we start ninth grade, and that's to get to the end of twelfth grade. Some people give themselves additional goals, like straight As or athletics. But that goal is sometimes really another goal in disguise—to get into a good college, where the goal of getting to the end just starts over. For some people, that's fine. They want to go to grad school or get a job that requires a specific degree, like counseling or pharmacy. If you need the degree, go after it. Don't let anything or anybody stand in your way. Like I said, that's fine for other people, but that wasn't for me. Though I did make it through college (Long Island University, Post), I encountered some of the same problems, and more besides.

Like I said, my issue with school wasn't with the idea of school itself. What I've come to understand is that it's hard to apply yourself when you're not passionate about what you're doing. If you don't do what you love, you're not going to be successful. In college, I did what was necessary, but not much more. I struggled to find the motivation to attend one particular class. I just could not get myself to go, but I needed to pass it. To solve that problem, I would get together with some of the other students, the ones I recognized as being at the top of the class, to study so I could pass the tests. It worked out well for me—I was able to see that I learned more from smaller groups and one-on-one interaction than I did sitting silently in a class.

So my issues really had to do not only with the process but also with passion. Exercise, hockey, business … these are things I'm passionate about. School, not so much. There are a lot of lessons they don't teach you in school. If I could do it all over, I wouldn't go to college. Instead, I would have jumped right into my own business. I knew I didn't want to be a doctor or a lawyer, and school wasn't the right place for me. Now, that's not to say that I see no value in school. It provides opportunities, after all, and it's a great place to establish connections. But it comes down to how you learn best, because make no mistake, you've got to learn a lot if you want to succeed as an entrepreneur. The key is to understand the type of learning environment that suits you. Some students only get by in school because they find the right teacher, someone who becomes a mentor. A one-on-one environment is more my style, and I've had some incredible mentors in my time. But beyond that, I learn by doing. I think things through, and then as I put plans into action, I learn as I go along. I'm not an abstract kind of guy, which may explain why school didn't work for me. I do better when I'm involved in an enterprise, on the ground and in the thick of it.

I also didn't like the power professors had over students. I remember one class I had to take three times because the professor kept failing me. I couldn't figure out why, since I kept up with all the work. I think it came down to the fact that he didn't like me. I did end up getting credit for the class. Eventually, he was investigated by the college, and he lost his job soon after I graduated.

As a teenager, I began to learn a valuable lesson, and a simple one: every no gets you closer to a yes! No matter your skills, no matter your connections, you've got to put in your time. We all get turned down. We all feel lost. Sometimes I think that's an important part of the process. Getting lost means you can find things. If you don't feel motivated or don't see the point in what you're doing, you've got to change your perspective. Figure out a goal that does motivate you, and find the right job to meet that goal. See your situation as an obstacle to overcome. School provides us with obstacles, and in that sense, there's something very valuable to it. But it also sets us up for problems, because eventually it ends. Once I got out of college, I had to invent a whole new type of job to accomplish my goals.

I like to say that you should be able to paint a picture of what you want out of life. Any journey you start, any goal you attain, it all starts with a vision. Nothing is impossible, and you've got to dream big. Like painting, a career takes patience and persistence. It also takes belief—belief that you can make the impossible possible. Think of painting as nothing more than a series of brushstrokes. You've got the vision in your head, and a blank canvas in front of you. If every no gets you closer to a yes, then each brushstroke, even one that goes astray, gets you closer to you realizing your vision.

My vision started with myself. I figured out what I wanted to be and what I wanted my life to be like, and then I did whatever it took to get there. For years, that involved getting up at three fifteen every morning, even when I had nothing else to do that day. My morning workout became a ritual, and without it, I was lost at sea. I was always driven, and that drive showed itself in my routines and rituals. We can rely on rituals to maintain ourselves. They put us in the right frame of mind to handle whatever the day throws at us. We establish our rituals when things are going well, and I think they help us keep going even when things get rough.

And life does get rough, no matter how successful you are. I've experienced plenty of ups and downs, and I've seen other people go through exactly the same struggles. That's one of my motivators: to make things a little less difficult for people who want to succeed, especially if they work for me. It's a foundational part of my vision.

3

WHO WANTS TO WORK FOR A BOSS?

Think about some simple facts: We spend about eight hours a day sleeping, eight hours a day working, and have eight hours a day to do everything else we need to do. That eight hours working usually doesn't include a commute, doesn't include meals or cooking, doesn't include bathing or cleaning or running errands. It doesn't include those things which happen during our free time, or when we'd rather be sleeping. That means that free time is the smallest portion of our day. And what do we do with that free time? We spend it with the people we love. So the people who matter most to us emotionally get the smallest chunk of time.

It turns out that the people we work with are often the ones we spend the most time with. So why would anybody want to work with people they can't stand? Work is already a stressful experience. You've got pressure to perform. With that in mind, I think you'd agree that it's better not to surround yourself with people who make things more stressful for you.

I got firsthand knowledge of how the wrong work environment can affect a person after I graduated from college. I had majored in business, so it seemed natural to get a job in a marketing firm.

Unfortunately, it wasn't long before I began to dread going to work every day. You see, I worked for a *boss*. He treated me like an employee. I know that doesn't sound all that bad, but think about it for a minute. We use the same term, *boss*, for something negative. Do you really want to be surrounded by people who can boss you around? The word *boss* comes from a Dutch word that means *master*, and I'm sure I don't have to go into the potentially negative meaning of that term. I knew right away that this job wasn't for me. Everyone was so negative that I couldn't stand it. I didn't want to be in that position. Why have a boss when you could be part of a family?

The negativity from that job leaked into my personal life. I hadn't been certain of what I wanted to do after college, but I soon became sure that I didn't want to work in such a negative environment. In other words, I didn't have a vision for my future, and I wasn't going to find it while I was working for a boss. That kind of hierarchy doesn't encourage a vision. Here's why: if your advancement is already laid out, if the ladder is in place, you've got no choice but to climb it. You can only go up and down. What if you want to go sideways? You can't—if you go sideways, you fall.

So what's the solution?

I admit that it took me a while to figure it out. I might not have figured it out if it weren't for a few things that fell into place. First, I couldn't stand the negativity. I was in marketing, which is all about sales, and it's easy to become cynical in that kind of environment. Speaking generally, sales isn't about improving the world; it's about making money. As you'll see, money's the last goal in my process. If you're chasing the money, you'll lose track of everything else that makes life worth living. If you want to change the world for the better, you've got to focus on helping people. If you can improve people's lives, you're going to improve your own life and sense of well-being. The money will come, but if that's all you're focused on, the money won't matter. A seven-figure salary won't make you happy if you're not making the world better while you're earning it. I learned these lessons by watching what was going on around me while I was working for a boss. Everybody was chasing that money. Marketing, sales … these things aren't the essential components of being an entrepreneur.

An entrepreneur is someone who undertakes an enterprise, an undertaking of some scope, complexity, and risk. The risks are financial first and foremost, but they can also be mental, emotional, and chronological. To be an entrepreneur, you have to have a lot of time to invest. Entrepreneurs are decision-makers who value self-reliance but also see how to make people of various talents work together toward a united goal. An enterprise is a business, yes, and it requires industrious effort. It's bold. It demands initiative. You've got to put yourself at stake. Nothing ventured, nothing gained; you've heard that before. You've got to be daring. And what comes from being daring? We call it adventure—excitement, suspense, and risk. To make it all work, you've got to be optimistic. If you can't imagine yourself succeeding, you never will. You won't be willing to take the necessary risks. And you won't be able to learn from mistakes.

I know what you're thinking—the risk might be too great. That's why I ultimately got out of marketing. Marketing is all about finding a market. It's about excluding people who might not want your business. I rejected that whole notion, and I found the perfect way to get around it. See, I don't exclude anybody. I think GYMGUYZ is for everybody. The only truly universal aspect of humanity is that we all have a body that needs to be kept fit.

That's why I want to redefine the whole concept of being an entrepreneur. Look it up in the dictionary. It means someone who organizes a business venture. Literally, we're told that it is all about undertaking business. And we all know what an undertaker is. That's not something I want to be involved in. My business is life. And anyway, that's not what the French words at the heart of entrepreneurship really mean. It comes from two words: *entre*, which means between, and *prendre*, which means to take. I didn't like that meaning, so I dug into the word a little more and found another one. It can also mean *to be successful*. And if you view success as I do, being successful means the opposite of taking—it means giving. What's the point of success if you can't share it? I don't just mean with your spouse and kids. I mean with the whole world.

Back to life after college … I didn't like my job and work environment. The culture was horrible. In truth, I was lost. I found myself driving around during my free time, not knowing what else to do. When I wasn't working, I was often taking naps, but not because I needed them. Sure, I was exhausted, but not physically. I was exhausted by the negativity around me and by the feeling that I wasn't on the right track. I'm as positive as they come, but my job was draining me.

After months of this marketing job, I knew I had to make a change. I wanted to be passionate about the work I did, and I couldn't feel that way about that marketing job. Since I'd always loved the fitness world, I decided to get back into it. I began moonlighting as a personal trainer at a gym.

The problem I now encountered was that I hadn't been working in months, so all my previous clients were no longer with me. A trainer without clients has the same problem as doctors without patients: they're essentially unemployed. The gym provided me with new clients. Sometimes they were late, sometimes they missed their appointments, and sometimes they cancelled. And one day, one of my clients showed up late for a training session. That might not seem like a life-changing event, but when she did show up, she said her workouts would be so much easier if I could just come to her house.

Boom.

GYMGUYZ!

What does that have to do with not working for a boss? Well, I'd learned a valuable lesson: what not to do. I didn't want to be a boss. I didn't want to surround myself with negativity and with people who hated being an employee. So I eliminated the boss-employee relationship. I don't have employees. I have a family. Here's what I mean by that: it's all about emotional intelligence.

Emotional Intelligence (EI) is so important that I build my business on it. Boiled down, it's the ability to understand people, how they want to be treated, and why we do what we do. It takes a lot of time to develop EI, though some people are lucky enough to be born with it. Components of EI are curiosity, insight, respect (the R in DRIVE; see chapter 9), and the ability to handle imperfection. People with high levels of EI understand themselves, their strengths and weaknesses. They are difficult to offend and are good at moving past their own mistakes. You see this kind of thing a lot in sports like hockey. A goalie who lets a puck get past him doesn't just give up. He's back on his feet, ready to deflect the next shot.

Here's another example. I was watching this woman talk to a clerk in a store. The clerk had made a mistake, and the woman was blowing up. She said, "What the hell are you doing? Is something wrong with you?" I couldn't believe it. You shouldn't talk to anyone like that. Blowing up at someone, yelling when somebody has made a mistake, tells everyone that you think you're better than the person who made the mistake. Now we're back to a hierarchy, and you already know how I feel about that. That woman thought she could talk that way to that sales clerk because she was higher up on the ladder. But what good did it do? Did it make her life better? No, of course it didn't. She only succeeded in making the clerk feel bad. People say that you should live without regrets, by which they mean that we regret the things that we didn't do and the risks we didn't take. Well, the angry woman in the store that day might disagree: my guess is that she came to regret the way she acted later on that day. We've got to respect each other.

That's emotional intelligence. It's your capacity for, first, understanding feelings—yours and other people's—and then determining what sort of emotion best fits the situation you're in at any moment. It's the ability to understand how people want to be treated. EI combines empathy with control. It's not repression, it's control. When you're interacting with other people, you've got to be aware not just of what you want but of what other people want and experience. You can probably see how this fits into the concept of a business as a family. If you're emotionally intelligent, you come to understand what makes a good work environment so that everyone can work effectively and efficiently.

EI plays out in a lot of different ways. Take the job interview as an example. I've conducted a lot of those, and my method is quite a bit different from the typical way experts recommend. I've heard people say to me that they've never been on an interview like ours. I grew up with this guy, and though we used to be best friends, I hadn't seen him in a long time. A while back he asked me a question about interviews. He wanted to know some good questions to ask a job candidate. I threw him off when I said that I always ask them what their favorite food is. Seems like exactly the wrong thing to ask, maybe, but I make it work. Once the candidate answers, I rephrase that question into the context of a dinner meal: If you went to a restaurant with executives, and something you ordered wasn't right, would you eat it or send it back? The thing is, there's no right or wrong answer—I'm not looking for them to say what I would say in that situation. The question lets me know how you perceive that kind of interaction. In answering it, you give me a glimpse into your thought process, how you'd handle yourself in a pressure situation when something unexpected happens. I'm all about behavioral stuff. I want to see how people are going to think in challenging situations. We need to gauge the candidate's response because that kind of situation will happen on the job, maybe not often, but it's unavoidable when you're dealing with other people in a professional capacity. At the end of the day, I want to empower people. I empower my team. I'm not a micromanager, constantly looking over someone's shoulder to make sure their method is in sync with mine. If you've got the skills, you're part of this family. Now go ahead and execute.

If you've got kids, you're probably aware of how hard it is to get children to do something they don't want to do, especially if they feel like it's not their job. Let's say you're having some people over to your house, and the place is a mess. You tell your son to clean up, and he says it's not his mess. He didn't leave the bowl of cheerios on the table, or didn't forget to take the laundry to the laundry room. You can get mad and yell at him to do what you say because you're the one who's in charge, or you can think about it emotionally. He doesn't realize that he's got something at stake in having a clean house. If it's his friend coming over, then he should want to clean up to make sure he knows where all his toys are so they can find them when they want them. If it's your friend, then you should make it clear that he's part of the family, and that involves helping each other out. It might not work right at that moment, but in having a family, you've got to think long-term. Your lesson might not work right then, but what about five years from now? The point of being a parent isn't to have someone to boss around. It's about making a grown-up who will succeed in the world twenty years from now.

With that in mind, I want you to understand that we don't just sell franchises; we award them. Yeah, it's a competition, but we don't compete: we win. If you want to be part of this family, first of all, you have to be the right fit. It really is like bringing in another family member. If you're a parent and your child is thinking about getting married to someone, you've got to evaluate the situation. Same thing with franchises. When considering a new franchisee, something I always like to ask myself is, would I want to have this person come regularly to my house for dinner? If the answer's no, if I'm not comfortable enough, then we don't award the franchise. You should like the people you surround yourself with and want them to be happy. And if you feel comfortable, if that feels like a good fit for them and the right fit for you, you move to the next step.

It's all about creating an environment where people are invested. Make them feel like they're part of a family, so they realize that if the family succeeds, they succeed. Here's an example. I had a meeting with a couple from Illinois who were looking to buy three franchises. Now, when you're in that situation, you can have everybody stroll in, sit around a table, and try to keep things light and casual. Not me. I have everyone line up in a straight line before the potential franchise family members come in, and I have my family greet them with a warm hello. When the married couple comes in, they're greeted, they're introduced. It's like a family reunion, or a wedding. The husband said to me, "I have to tell you, when I came in yesterday I felt like I was talking to friends in my kitchen." That's the culture you want to have.

This is the sort of thing that a lot of people would say is good management. I don't like to use the word *manage*. That implies that my family members are not really accountable, that it's all on me. I hold everyone accountable, which means that I trust them to know what they need to know to be able to get the job done. Let's say you're in my family, and you've got your time off set at sixteen days a year, but suddenly you need one more day off. If you're on my team, that means I trust you. What, am I going to dock your pay? To me, doing so would be to ignore the lessons of emotional intelligence. Your job as an entrepreneur is to know every one of your family members. You make it so you trust them, and they can trust you.

I cringe whenever someone calls me a boss. I could throw up from it. I hate it. People ask, what do we call you? They call me "our fearless leader." But that's not the end of it. I may be a leader, but at GYMGUYZ, everyone's a leader. I don't care if someone's been on board for a day or ten years. They're all important members of the family. Every single Monday, I find out what everyone did over the weekend—how people's kids are, things like that. I know their kids' names. I check in. I make sure everyone's okay. If I create an environment where people feel uncomfortable talking to me or asking me a question, I've failed. I was talking to one of my development guys on the phone.

He asked me to send an email and then apologized, saying, "I shouldn't be asking the CEO to send an email."

I said, "Why not?"

How many people would be comfortable to ask the CEO for something like that? He did, even though he thought it was a mistake. I'd created an environment where it was okay, and that has always been my goal.

The night after meeting with the married couple about the new franchises, one of my team members sent an email to the entire family that said, not even thinking about it, "I love you all." You might think that's an odd thing to appear in a company-wide email. But the best thing happened because of it. All of a sudden, a chain of emails came in, saying, "I love you too" and "We love each other." Without a high level of EI, an entrepreneur can't make something like that happen. And I consider it a real sign of success.

THE VISION

I get up pretty early, long before the sun's up. I've been like that for a long time. Even when I was younger and had nothing else to do, I'd bike seven miles to the gym and back at four thirty every day. It seems crazy to me, and I couldn't have told you exactly why I did it at the time. Now, I see it as nothing more than part of my personality, and I consider it one of my strengths. I've always been good at managing my time. When everything else seemed designed to beat me down, I relied on routines like my morning workout to keep me on my feet.

Everybody's got strengths and weaknesses. Everybody's got areas of expertise. Some people are lucky and get paid millions of dollars doing something they can do without effort. But for everybody else, it's all about a journey to becoming good at something. There are lots of people out there giving advice about how to succeed and how to be an entrepreneur. Here's my advice: to succeed, you've got to start with a vision. It's the same thing that a painter does when looking at a blank canvas. Painters can paint anything they want. They've got the canvas, the brush, and the paint, and no limitations beyond their own imagination. But they can't paint anything if they don't have a vision. If they can't point their imagination in a specific direction, they'll stand there all day staring at a blank canvas. Before that first brush stroke can intrude on the white canvas, there needs to be a vision in the painter's mind of what the final picture will look like. Fill the mind before filling the canvas.

So, how can you fill your mind? Here's how I did it: I paid attention. It all started with that job I got after college. Like I said in the last chapter, that negativity was getting me down, and I knew that I couldn't let it continue. What I needed to do was what I'd already been doing my whole life: I sliced that negative (-) down the center (|) and made it positive (+). If I hadn't been paying attention to that client who wished for a more convenient workout—by which I mean that if I'd been mired in negativity and annoyed by the fact that she was late—GYMGUYZ might never have happened, and I wouldn't be writing this book right now. I didn't let my mood get me down. Of course, it's not that simple; the idea isn't complicated, but the execution is, just like painting a picture.

Without the idea, there's nothing to execute. But without execution, the idea is worthless. There are lots of ways to demonstrate this, but let's stick with the idea of painting to think this through. Let's take as our model the person standing in front of a blank canvas, a palette full of colors in the crook of his thumb. It's endless possibility, right? Now, to some people, that can be daunting. Without any direction, it's hard to get started. That's why a plan is so important, and why so many people get discouraged and never finish what they start. You've got to be able to see it, feel it, and believe it.

Despite the internet, people still go to museums to see art. The reason is simple: no image on a screen is as rich and beautiful as seeing its original form. Paintings have texture as a result of their physical form, the way that paint is layered on canvas. It's vibrant in ways a digital image can't reproduce. That's not to disparage computers. I just want to point out that each kind of art has its own strengths and that a good artist will take advantage of them. When you stand in the same room as an original painting, it's a different experience. And that's part of why museums are still around. It's also why I want to have a close relationship with all of my GYMGUYZ family members. I teach them to reproduce the painting with actual paint, not just to take a photograph of it. I strive to get them to the point where they've mastered the techniques, so they can do it too.

So here's how to create your vision: Start with the idea that there are many different types of painting. You don't have to conform to the way we see reality. You can be a cubist like Pablo Picasso or a surrealist like Salvador Dali if you want. Me? I'm all about perspective, and I wanted to create a vision so detailed and nuanced that it might as well be the real thing. (In the art world, it's called trompe l'oeil—a painting so realistic that it makes the viewer think it's the real thing. Illusions like that are big on the internet these days.) That's how an awful lot of paintings are made, with a nod toward reality. That means the painter is painting from a specific viewpoint, with some objects foreshortened and others diminished so that the whole thing looks three-dimensional. And the way to start that kind of painting is to put the objects farthest away on the canvas first.

In painting the GYMGUYZ picture, even back when it was just something in my own head, that meant the plan was to franchise it from day one. Everything else flows from that decision. To understand GYMGUYZ, you've got to understand my idea of success. I can't stress this enough: It's not just about money. Sure, money's nice, but it's just a means to an end. As an entrepreneur, I've always wanted to make people's lives better— that's the true measure of success. And I'm not just talking about the people I know or my own local community. Right away, I looked as far into the future as I could. What's the end goal of GYMGUYZ? It's worldwide availability. I wanted to create the number-one fitness brand in the world, providing for the needs of the greatest possible number of people. And the best way to accomplish that was to open up the opportunity for franchising.

One way in which an entrepreneur resembles a painter is that both careers can be lonely. Paintings aren't done by committee. Painters are solitary by nature, and an entrepreneur might be like that, especially at the beginning. And with both careers, there's that moment when you've got to unveil your work to other people. When you put it out there for everybody to see, you also put yourself out there, and you've got to be emotionally ready for rejection. You have to be ready because it's going to happen.

Still, you've got to put it out in the world. Sure, you can paint pictures solely for your own benefit, but being an entrepreneur isn't like that. For your business to succeed, you've got to share it. Like art, it's something you create, so it's a part of you. By being ready, I mean that even though it's a part of you, you can't take it personally when others don't share your vision. I may wish everybody I talked to early on had joined me in GYMGUYZ, but I respect their decision not to.

As I was starting to envision GYMGUYZ, I was training a tremendously successful guy—a billionaire. I looked up to him, to say the least, and I told him my plan. I painted my picture for him, laid it all out there. He told me that I was wasting my time and it would never work. That punch was hard to roll with, and I never forgot it. I could have gotten mad at him, cut ties with him, and moved on, but that's not the right way to respond. It's no use to hold a grudge. Instead, I decided to prove him wrong.

As Walt Disney liked to say, "It's kind of fun to do the impossible." Now, I think a lot of people consider it impossible to create a new category, to do something that's never been done before. We tend to think that everything's been done already. The people who innovate are idolized. We try to imitate them by doing what they do. In painting, it was artists like Claude Monet who rejected the styles popular in the nineteenth century and set up their own exhibit. When that happened, people who didn't like what they were doing called them Impressionists. They meant it as an insult, but it became a huge force in the art world. The Impressionists couldn't be stopped. The result was a flood of imitators. Those imitations often pale by comparison because they got the lesson wrong. The true imitators wouldn't have been impressionists—they wouldn't have painted in the same way that Monet did. They'd have come up with their own new style. They'd have created a new category. Well, we created a new category, a type of business that never existed until GYMGUYZ began. I think that's why so many people thought like that billionaire client I trained. When something's too different, it seems impossible, or maybe even worthless. We're the first in the world to offer customized in-home personal training. Because it was so different, it took a lot of time, hard work, and believing.

Belief is important any time you do something difficult. If you don't believe it can happen, you're never going to make it happen. In my opinion, you've got to approach your enterprise with zero doubt that it's going to work. Don't leave room in the back of your mind for contingency plans. Give your vision 100 percent of your mental energy and creativity. Back to art: You'll never hear an artist say that what he or she is painting won't work out. Da Vinci never said, "If I can't get the Mona Lisa to look right, I'll just paint houses for a living." As soon as you put in your mind the idea of a backup plan, you're going to fail. That's a guarantee. I never started this thinking to myself, *If this doesn't work, it's not a problem. I can always get a job at a gym again.* I knew right away that I was going to do this for the rest of my life, and that's exactly what I'm doing.

In other words, don't build failure into your business model. That doesn't mean you shouldn't be realistic. Of course people fail, and of course things are beyond your control. The only thing that really matters is how you deal with these obstacles. You've got to anticipate and compensate. Anticipate: figure out what might go wrong or could potentially be defective. Compensate: make up for those defects, both *before* they happen and *as* they happen. Painters do this by planning ahead. A lot of painters sketch the layout of the finished painting before they even set up an easel. They figure out what goes where first, so there aren't any big surprises. They figure out practical elements of the finished work. Where's the light coming from? Where's the viewer standing? How far away are those mountains in the background? It seems simple, like anybody would know how to do it without thinking, but it's not. It requires a lot of thought and imagination, but it doesn't hurt to combine those with experience and technical knowledge.

You can also think of it like plotting a mystery novel. You start with the murder, understanding the criminal's motivation, and then you work backward through the clues and to the detective.

Starting with the things in the distance, I imagined GYMGUYZ as a worldwide phenomenon. I still say it to myself every day: worldwide. I knew it would be hard. It takes work to make it work. But I believed from day one that it was going to happen. I see that picture in my mind. And now we're moving outside the United States into Canada. Give it five years and we'll be in at least five countries, maybe even more. It only started because I believed in it.

Being an entrepreneur begins with belief, and it continues with obsession. I eat, sleep, and breathe GYMGUYZ. All I wear is GYMGUYZ. As I like to say: I sweat red every day. You need to be in it, you need to feel it, and you need to see it. I'm certainly not the only one who thinks about things this way. The actor Jim Carrey tells a story about the very same thing. Back before he made it big as an actor, he would visualize his own idea of success, which for him included being offered roles in big films and working with great directors. He took this vision and made it concrete when he wrote himself a check for $10 million "For acting services rendered," dated several years down the line. He put the check in his wallet, where it deteriorated but never disappeared. Then he got the role for one of the leads in *Dumb and Dumber*, which got him ten million.

When Jim Carrey told that story, which I first heard when I was watching a YouTube video of him on *The Oprah Winfrey Show*, he was quick to point out that the visualization isn't enough—you've got to work at it. That's true in business, and it's especially true when it comes to personal fitness. It's not just the exercise itself that's hard. You've also got to make time for it. Planning your days, that's work too, and if you don't maintain it, your schedule can become flabby. And even if you do it right, it's never over. There's always a new day, a new temptation to slack off or take the easy route. With GYMGUYZ, I envisioned success as something that's never-ending. Never done. You will always continue to improve.

One issue I've dealt with in fitness is that after a while, a person's motivation can decrease. Motivation is key to improvement over the long term. That's why we don't merely set up a routine for our clients; we also provide motivation. Our coaches are in the room with the client. It's so much easier when there's someone there constantly helping you reach your goals, even redefining those goals. You're always going to want to be better, right?

This kind of continually bettering yourself is another area where fitness and business overlap. There's always room for improvement. You want to keep your business continually growing. The trick is to understand your goals. That's why I wanted to make sure my assessment procedure was precise. If you want to be an entrepreneur, you've got to understand your resources. I applied that logic to fitness. We start with a three-pronged assessment that examines our clients' body, nutrition, and fitness. No one really spends enough time on understanding the whole person. It's important to communicate with the clients so they understand the process. That way they can improve in ways that extend beyond their physical condition.

As I said, success means improving people's lives. I want to make a difference. There's an important but unstated element that I want to make clear: my vision of success isn't just about my clients; it's also about my GYMGUYZ family. For my clients, I want to change the way they feel about their bodies and improve their health. For my GYMGUYZ family, I want to give them the opportunity to thrive in their careers. That's just as true with the franchise family members as it is with the people I see in the office every day. I love hearing how people have changed their lives by becoming part of this family. We meet annually at our conference, and we've begun posting their stories on our YouTube channel. A lot of our franchisees come from very different backgrounds, but a large proportion of them are fitness fanatics. Once they're able to pursue their passion, to incorporate it into their career, their behavior changes. They're excited to get up in the morning. If you love your job, then your whole life is going to improve. That's right: being a part of GYMGUYZ is going to improve your life, no matter what role you take. Client, coach, franchise family member—there's something for everybody.

We've covered seeing and believing, so let's get to feeling. The key concept here is texture. Think of texture as the physical equivalent of depth in a painting, its three-dimensional quality. We say something has texture when it's not smooth or flat. In other words, it's got details. Give your vision details. Nothing should be hazy. Remember that trompe l'oeil: make it so real you can almost touch it.

When I started, I mapped out what success would look like. I tried to figure out how long it was going to take me and obviously, how much money I would need. People say you can't start a business with no money. That's not entirely true. You do need some money, but probably not as much as you think. The tough part financially really begins when you start to grow. That's when you've got to figure out how to bring in the revenue you need. You can start with little, but you're not going to grow without money. That's just the bottom line.

I didn't have money. I didn't come from a rich family. My family life growing up was average. I didn't always get everything I wanted. I grew up playing hockey, and I remember wanting an actual hockey bag to carry all my gear in. But we couldn't spend the money to buy me a hockey bag, so I had to carry all my equipment in two smaller bags, which is more of a hassle than it seems. The way I was brought up definitely taught me the value of things and how to appreciate what you've got. When I developed GYMGUYZ, I saved up fifteen grand to get started.

My expenses weren't all that big. I produced some flyers, got together some portable exercise equipment, and calculated about how much I'd have to spend on gas. I gave myself two weeks to make it work. I did have some help, of course. I worked out of my parents' house, at their dining room table. My brother Jason stepped up when I needed him. And I got to work driving around all day, drumming up business, finding clients, and making them sweat.

GYMGUYZ had begun.

After those first two weeks were up, I knew it was going to work. Demand was huge.

Remember that billionaire I mentioned, the one who said my vision was impossible? He stayed on as a client for a while, but soon his schedule became overloaded to the point that he couldn't keep training with us. Two years after I stopped training him, I awarded the first GYMGUYZ franchise. Six months ago, as I write this, we were ranked one of the top franchises in the world. He called me up one day not too long ago and said, "I was wrong. Congratulations, very impressive."

Fuel

As I was starting out, I'd often get out that paintbrush to describe the vision. I'd show people where I was going, and so many of them didn't believe me. I just wish they did, because then they might have become a part of GYMGUYZ.

5

EXECUTION

Now you've got your vision. You've refined it in your mind and are able to imagine both background and foreground. You know your ultimate goal as well as what you need to do right now to start making it real. You've even dipped the brush in the paint. Now you've got to put the paint on the canvas. That can be a terrifying moment.

I want to switch things up a little bit. Instead of thinking of an entrepreneur as a painter, let's think of an entrepreneur as a doctor. It might seem like an odd comparison at first, but remember back to chapter 1 and the similarity between doctors and trainers—a trainer without clients is just as unemployed as a doctor without patients. When it comes down to it, there's almost no difference between the goals of both these professions. They both work toward the health of those they serve. It's not just about fixing the immediate problem; it's about lifestyle.

Let's say you go in to see a doctor because you've got back pain. There's an easy solution: the doctor could prescribe pain medication and send you on your way. But no doctor worth visiting is going to do that. There has to be more to it than just treating the symptoms. They've got to find the cause. To do so, they're going to take a look at your lifestyle and find the behavior or event that caused the pain in order to prescribe the best method to get rid of it. The treatment might include a lifestyle change, safety precautions, addressing other problems (like the way you sleep), or any one of a hundred different things at the root of the issue. Of course there are going to be cases where the patient was involved in an accident that caused it, but even then the prescription will be for physical therapy rather than just hoping for the best.

Trainers operate the same way. Let's say the client sets up a free visit with one of our coaches because they feel like they need to lose weight. It's easy enough to say, "Exercise and change your diet to reduce your daily amount of calories." As if anything is ever that easy. We need to get to the cause of the situation in the first place. Sometimes you've got to attend to mental conditions as well as physical.

That's not to say that we're providing psychiatric counseling. We're not in that business, of course. But we do administer our three assessments: body, nutrition, and fitness. We look at your body. We review your medical history, take your weight (including body fat percentage, muscle mass percentage, body mass index, visceral fat, and body age), and your inch measurements. We take a look at your strength, endurance, flexibility, and balance. And importantly, we discuss your goals. Some people have only a vague idea of what they want out of training. They might say that they want to "feel better" or "get healthier" so they can live longer. Others have very specific things they want. They might be having children and want to be able to care for them. They might want to be able to hike up mountains or run a marathon. As a patient, what do you want to get out of your visit to the doctor? As a client, what do you want to get out of your sessions with our coaches? And as an entrepreneur, how do you define your success? In other words, what do you want to see in the picture you're painting? Even if you don't think these questions are hard, it's worth devoting some thought to them.

I wanted to be satisfied with my work. I wanted to make a difference, make people's lives better. I also wanted to be a financial success. Those elements are all related, but they're not exactly the same thing. Yes, I could be satisfied with the work I was doing and not be successful at it. Think of that difference as the same thing that happens if you're, say, a writer. You might derive great satisfaction from sitting down for an hour a day and writing in a journal or making up a story. That doesn't mean you're successful. What if nobody reads them? Still satisfying, but no success. I could also make a difference without tying it to my career. I could do volunteer work, donate to charities. But I wanted all these things tied together. Success is to be shared. And that's how I envisioned GYMGUYZ. I wanted it to help people who need it. So we've got our GYMGUYZ Gives programs, including our Confidence Campaign. In 2016, we began working directly with schools (and through our franchises, we're able to reach communities nationwide) to combat bullying by building children's confidence. That's why worldwide is so important. The more people GYMGUYZ can reach, the more resources we have to continue to make a difference. The GYMGUYZ philosophy is simple: Amazing approach … amazing results.

You can probably see how this relates to developing a vision, as described in chapter 4. Your vision is all about goals. Quantify them. I set goals that are easy to express: Right now, I want to have five hundred franchises in the next five years.

Once your goals are clear, you can start setting into motion your plan for reaching those goals. I knew in the beginning that

GYMGUYZ wouldn't be able to go worldwide if we couldn't even get the word out to the people in my area. Distributing flyers was a good beginning, but it was never going to be enough. I would drive up and down the Long Island Expressway just to make visible our red van with GYMGUYZ plastered along the side.

I knew I needed to get the word out, and there's always a way, even if it costs gas money.

I kept at it every day, trying to spread the word through any means I could find. I would go to an exclusive, high-end shopping center and hand out flyers. I was there so much that security told me I couldn't stay because I wasn't a shopper. I got around this by collecting bags from the stores in the shopping center, which I filled with business cards and flyers and carried around so I could look like I was supposed to be there. I became friendly with the employees there and got even more opportunities to advertise. At other places I would set up a table so people could see our name and I could distribute business cards. I treated it like I was at a business convention, handing out cards for free sessions to get people's attention.

Fuel

I'm not saying these techniques are going to work for everyone, nor that they're even advisable. I just want to show you what it takes. There's always a way. You've got to figure out how to execute. When I needed cash, I would sell things I had around the house—sports cards, hockey equipment, whatever I had. I'd go to local shops, find buyers online. Every little bit helps.

It also helps to be consistent. Every Sunday my dad and I would, from four in the morning until noon, go from house to house to deliver flyers. (On a side note: don't put these in mailboxes. Those are federal property, and only mail can go in them. I found that out the hard way, after hours of work. Frustration comes with the territory.)

But there's a reason people see a bump in sales after a television commercial airs. Here's how I got to talk about GYMGUYZ on TV. It's about being different, and it's about persistence. First, I took a look at what kinds of shows might be open to doing a segment on our operation. Lots of local news outlets and morning shows will devote time to local services they think their viewers might be interested in. The trick was, of course, getting their attention. I learned which reporters did the kinds of stories that I was interested in telling. I picked one, contacted her a few times, but got no response. But I kept at it. I knew where the station was headquartered, and when she arrived and left every day. Before too long, I learned that every morning she went to a doughnut shop to get her coffee. I had to do something, so I asked the woman at the counter in the coffee shop what the reporter ordered. So when she came in the next morning I was waiting for her with the coffee she always ordered. It was maybe a bit of a risk, but it worked. She heard me out, and I got on the air.

Sometimes that's all it takes. You get your foot in the door, and other opportunities open up. We've since been showcased on other networks, been featured in magazines like *People* and *Forbes,* and we have had our story told in the *New York Times.*

The punchline here is simple: know your business. As an entrepreneur, you should never go into anything blind. Figure out where you fit into the rest of the world. My place, as I knew even when I was a teenager, is within the world of personal training, but as an entrepreneur I knew I didn't want to open up another gym. Sure, gyms help people, but I'd learned from my own experience that the kind of help they offer isn't going to fit everyone's needs. A centralized location requires a kind of effort that a lot of people can't put forth. There's too much in the way. In my view, a gym makes it too easy to avoid your workout. Sure, I emphasize convenience, but it's more than that: it's a type of commitment that you have to actively avoid. It's easy not to go to the gym; it's not so easy when a coach shows up at your door.

Think of being an entrepreneur in that way. There's an old piece of advice that fits here, and it has to do with waking up to an alarm clock. Most people put their clock right next to their bed. That way, it's easy to fling your arm out and hit the snooze button. Instead, why not put the alarm across the room? Once it starts buzzing, you've got to get up to turn it off. You're already on your feet, the blood's pumping strong, and you're more likely to stick to your schedule. Being an entrepreneur is hard enough, so don't make it easy to avoid. I mentioned last chapter that you shouldn't paint failure into your vision, and little things like this can help you prevent it.

So remember to focus, to engage, to execute, none of which are things you can do once and leave at that. Back to doctors: they have staff members who make sure you schedule follow-up appointments. If something's wrong with you, they put in place a mechanism to make sure you're improving. They have their staff call you, and they bring you back in a week or two later to see how you're doing. As an entrepreneur, you've got to do the same thing: that is, follow through. A while back I gave a speech to a group of aspiring entrepreneurs, and afterward a lot of them came up to me and asked me if they could call me or email me. You know how many of them did? Zero. Not a single one. Now, maybe they're the kind of people who will go on to great success, but I guarantee it won't happen unless they follow up. They began well, by asking for help and advice. I'm all for finding mentors—I wouldn't be where I am without the help I got from others, and now I'm thrilled to be in the position to help people. But you've got to follow through.

There is a reason why that event—the fact that nobody got in touch with me—was so disappointing, and it's something a lot of people don't think about very often: teachers love to have great students. If you talk to an elementary school teacher, you'll quickly find out why they do what they do. It's day in, day out wrangling kids into the room, into line, into their desks. It's a tough job. Everybody knows that part. So how do they get through it year after year? Simple. They survive because of the one student who grows and learns, who changes throughout the class, who blossoms. One student can make a year feel like it's worth the effort, that the teacher isn't wasting his or her time. It's the same with our coaches; if one client's life improves, then we're accomplishing our goals. Go to our website and you'll see testimonies to the power of our approach to personal training. We call them transformations, and they're why we do what we do.

Put that element into your vision as you paint it. You'd better believe that doctors do it. Helping people, no matter the scale, makes our time here valuable. Don't chase the money, chase the vision, and it'll work out.

If you look at our transformations page on our website, you'll see lots of before and after photos. That's standard for people in our field, of course. So here's where focusing, engagement, and executing are vital. In a lot of cases, the after pictures don't last long. Soon, you're back to the same condition you were in before you started. I'm reminded of the difficulties people face when trying to lose weight on the show *The Biggest Loser*. Here's a show produced by people who truly want to do some good in the world, but they're hindered by their format. They have trainers to look after their contestants for the entire production, and they accomplish some amazing things during that time. Then the show's over and all the contestants go home. Without the support of the show behind them, a lot of the contestants return to their original weight. This isn't difficult to explain: keeping off weight, especially weight lost in a really short amount of time (such as the length of the show's production schedule), is really, really hard. Our bodies *try* to gain the weight back. That's why you've got to maintain your regimen.

On top of that difficulty, it's all too easy to take a break once you've reached a goal. That break can sometimes be a good thing. Lay back and enjoy your success. But you've got to be careful, or the break you're on becomes the new status quo, and before you know it, you're right back where you started. After two weeks, your muscles begin to weaken (this is called the detraining principle). That's why the GYMGUYZ mission is never complete. We keep showing up every day, focused on not only reaching the goal, but surpassing it. Let's say your goal is to lose twenty pounds. Once you get there, now what? You've got to set new goals. You've lost twenty pounds? Great, now the real work begins. Stay engaged and keep the weight off. You ran a marathon? Great. Now do it again next year.

I apply this line of thinking to my career. GYMGUYZ became my full-time job. Great, now start hiring coaches. Now franchise. Now go international. Hire more coaches, so they can make money doing something that makes them feel good and is valuable to the world. Help more clients meet their goals. Work with schools to handle bullying. Sponsor a charity.

Success is not given; it's earned. You've got to execute. That means finding a way to make things work when it seems impossible. It's fun to do the impossible. That doesn't mean you have to do it on your own. I like to say that you need to be able to be friends with a criminal, and you need to be able to be friends with a millionaire. If you can be friends with both, then you can be very successful. It shows that you have the ability to adapt and be comfortable in any situation.

The mentality of a billionaire and the mentality of a criminal are going to be very different. And it's not enough just to get through a meeting with a couple of people on the opposite ends of the personality spectrum. Being a friend means that your relationship is more than superficial. It means you know each other well, and it means you can trust them and rely on them. Not only that: it means they trust you. Doctors demonstrate this kind of adaptability all the time. They don't pick their patients based on personality. Instead, they decide what kind of medicine they want to pursue: general practice, surgery, urology, gastroenterology. Their specialization has nothing to do with the kinds of people they will treat, only with their expertise. Sure, some people go into surgery because they don't want to have to do primary care, but the surgeons still meet with the patients before and after the surgery. And that means they'll have to tailor their interactions to the individual. They have to read people, get to know them, and figure out how to treat them in effective ways—we're back to emotional intelligence. Believe me—that means adapting to different personalities. That's pretty much what it is in business. I can talk to anyone and be able to be friends with him or her in ten minutes. If you can adapt, you can be very successful. If you have the ability to adapt your personality to get along with most every kind of person in the world, you will win.

If you've got a product to sell or a service to provide, you want to reach as many people as possible with it. What does it matter what their personality is like? You're meeting a need. I chose training because that field fits with who I am and have always been. But regardless of the work I chose to do, I kept in mind the need to be versatile. I had to have a different mind-set for different tasks. For a while it was just me: coach, clerk, advertiser, driver, account manager, networker. But things got bigger. Just like doctors rely on nurses, clerical staff, and technicians, so entrepreneurs have to learn to rely on people.

In the beginning, I had family. My parents provided me a place to get started. My brother Jason stepped up and helped me out. I'd go to conferences and shows where I'd have to demo our service, so I needed someone to do the routine with me. I'd stand up on stage and show the audience what GYMGUYZ was, and Jason was right there with me, doing the routine, embodying the vision.

As time went on, I built my own family. I brought in coaches, which meant I could focus on scalability and realizing the vision. I brought in a staff to handle the business end of things, especially when we got into franchising. And before too long, I even found a wife, who has been so supportive. I'm thankful that I have her. She understands.

THE STRUGGLE

You've painted your vision.

You've set things in motion.

Now what?

Honestly, now you're going to have to struggle.

You'll probably make mistakes.

You're going to get turned down.

It's inevitable. Failure and difficulties can define you if you let them. Or you can be defined by how you respond to them. If you think, "They said no, so that's it," you'll never get anywhere. Instead, say to yourself, "Every no gets me closer to a yes." It's almost like we've all got to put in our time and face a certain amount of adversity before we can succeed. We have to make a certain number of mistakes before things work right. That's not true, of course, but thinking of the process in that way can help you get through it.

I started making mistakes pretty early in the GYMGUYZ process. There are too many to count. Some of them are the kinds of things you do when you're tired, stressed out, and have way too much to think about. One example that comes to mind happened when I got business cards. After I picked up and paid for them, I noticed that I'd forgotten to put the address for the website on them. I had to pay to reprint all of them. Mistakes often result from rushing or happen because you're not thinking things through. Never act on impulse.

One time I wasted a whole day at the DMV because I didn't have one of the documents that was important in registering a GYMGUYZ van. That's an easy thing to correct, but it can still take all day. With something like that, all you have to do is make a list, and you can even check it against the requirements listed at the DMV website.

The important thing is to learn from your mistakes, which is the only way to make them worthwhile. Don't let them get you down, because everybody makes them. Never forget: nobody's perfect. I think of mistakes like they're sore muscles. If you're working out, you could do exactly the same set every day, with exactly the same intensity. The problem with that method is that you'll never improve. So you have to work out according to the overload principle. It's necessary to overload your muscles in order to make them stronger. Push yourself, and you'll see improvement. If your workout starts to seem too easy, then it's time to add another set, time to shave a few seconds off your mile time or add another ten pounds to your curls.

Overloading your muscles make them hurt, at least at first. There's some discussion as to why this happens: either it's the result of lactic acid building up (the older theory) or it's because of small tearing in the muscles that happen when you use them a lot. Whatever the cause, exercising to improve your body is going to hurt. The same goes for starting a business. There's going to be pain at first, though it can take many forms. For me, it was the pain of going without some things, sacrifices I had to make in terms of food and free time. Pain also took the form of rejection, and above all, it came in the form of mistakes. Learning from mistakes can be as difficult as it is to correct them, but it's equally as important. It's difficult because it requires reflection. You've got to think hard about what you've done and how you can do it differently next time.

Sometimes, something you do might seem like a mistake, but it still accomplishes your goal. I heard this big-time business guy was having a meeting. I had to get an invitation, and to do that, I knew I needed to stand out, make myself memorable. My solution: I went to the corporate headquarters wearing a sweatshirt and a pair of shorts. I didn't even have an appointment. I just walked in and started talking to the woman at the front desk. I got on her good side, and she was kind enough to point me to the right room. I opened the door to the conference room, and everybody sitting there turned their heads, looking at me. They had no idea how to respond, so one of them said, "How can we help you?" I said I was very excited to see them, and I told them what I wanted. They'd never seen anyone come in like that. I had their attention, and I knew what to do with it.

Even if you somehow avoid making mistakes, that doesn't mean things are going to go smoothly. You've still got to deal with bumps in the road. And believe me: no matter what road you pick—entrepreneur, artist, doctor—there will be bumps. No road is paved perfectly.

In part, things become hard simply because you're dealing with paperwork, so there's always the danger of overlooking something important, like the forms for the DMV. Then there are tax forms, payroll, scheduling, advertising … My advice: hire an accountant.

In part, things become difficult simply because you're dealing with other people. People are unpredictable, and that's why I've

51

stressed the need for versatility and emotional intelligence in your interactions. You've got to be able to handle it when people come up short and make decisions you don't agree with. Consider this example: I was building the business in its early stages. One Sunday night at eight o'clock, I got a call from a new coach who said he couldn't do it anymore. No two weeks' notice, no warning. The job wasn't for him, so he just quit, right then on the phone. I had a panic attack because he had eight sessions the next day, and I had eight sessions the next day. How was I going to get all these sessions in? How was I going to make it to all the different locations? I spent three hours that night going over maps and time frames, figuring out how I could make it all work. I knew it was important not to cancel sessions, because once you do that, your clients lose trust in you. I arranged for some clients to go to each other's houses for group sessions. I asked others to meet at different locations so I wouldn't have to be late because of drive time. And I asked my brother to help me.

Beyond having reliable people on your side (and as clients), as an entrepreneur you've got to be able to handle rejection. The amount of times I've been told no … I can't even count that high. I've been told no more times than you can imagine. To handle it, I never looked it as a rejection, certainly not one that meant my effort was for nothing. In the beginning I was trying to build my name in the area, and I wanted to get on this local news station. I mentioned this in the previous chapter, that I'd communicated with reporters in every way possible—email, phone, mail, you name it. With a situation like that, I had to think outside the box and change it up.

As I've mentioned, every no gets you closer to a yes. You hear stories about people dealing with what we might think of as crushing amounts of rejection, yet they persevere. You know who you don't hear about? The people who give up. J. K. Rowling, who wrote the Harry Potter books, got rejection letters from dozens of agents and publishers. She'd written other books before that one too, and they were all rejected. She didn't let that stop her. She finished her Harry Potter books and could have lived her life any way she wanted. She never had to work again. You know what she did? She kept writing. That's the kind of persistence you need to be an entrepreneur.

Take Steve Jobs as another example. He got fired from Apple, the company he created. How did he respond? He had resources, so he bought a little company called Pixar. He also started a new computer company called NeXT. That one didn't pan out as well as Pixar did, but he didn't let that stop him. He stuck with it, and soon enough Apple bought NeXT. He was back at his company, where he soon took over as CEO. Apple was floundering, but Steve Jobs didn't let that bother him. Now we have the iPhone, and by 2012, Apple was the most valuable company in the United States. It's consistently in the top ten companies in the world.

Monumental struggles are typical in the business world. I remember one night having a panic attack because I had to make payroll the next week but I didn't have the funds available. I could put together maybe $10,000, but I needed more than twice that to make it. I was desperate, to the point that I was thinking about going to a casino and putting everything on red. Fortunately, my head cleared and I came up with some other ideas. I got on the phone, calling as many clients as possible and offering specials, freebies, anything I could think of to get some money coming in. I wound up amassing $40,000, almost twice what I needed to make payroll. Anything's possible if you're willing to put in the effort, develop emotional intelligence, and keep a clear head.

One of the biggest problems I encountered early on had to do with trying to park the van. Without a centralized office, we didn't have a set spot for parking. I kept the van parked in an open lot. One night, we had a huge snowstorm. When I got to the lot the next morning, I couldn't see the van. The parking lot was completely plowed clean after the storm had ended, but the workers decided to dump all the snow on our van. It was buried. It took me about six and a half hours to dig it out. I still don't know why they did that. Obviously, I never parked the van there again.

But that wasn't the end of the van problems. I rented a parking spot from a woman who lived nearby. One night my phone rang at two o'clock. The woman who owned the spot was on the line, whispering to me that she thought someone was breaking into the van. She had looked out her window and seen a light on in the van, so she assumed somebody was trying to steal it. That van was my livelihood, so I jumped out of bed, grabbed a baseball bat, and drove over to the spot. Turns out, nobody was trying to break in. One of the coaches had left the door open—that was all. But it was already three in the morning and I had a client to meet in fifteen minutes, so I just went to work.

Another problem with the van: One morning I arrived at the bakery where I kept it parked, only to find that someone had blocked it in with their van. I ran from building to building in the area trying to find out whose van it was. I ended up finding the guy in a hockey rink but only after going to both benches. He told me I could get the keys from the locker room, but initially he told me the wrong place to find them, so I had to run back and get the right information. That took up precious time that morning, but I got to my sessions. I hate being late to sessions, and I hated even more to cancel them, especially at the last minute. But I did what I had to do to get on the road.

Fuel

Sometimes I had packed my schedule with so many meetings and sessions that I didn't even have time to go home at the end of the day. I kept a pack with a toothbrush and things like that with me so I could sleep in the van if I had to. One time that came in handy because I had early sessions one day but also wanted to meet with a reporter. I showered and got everything ready the night before and went to the location so I was ready first thing. I was on time for the meeting that morning, which enabled me to get our story in a magazine. Looking back, I think it might have been best to eliminate my apartment altogether as all I did was sleep there. I didn't have time for anything else, as I was consumed with work.

There are going to be troubles you won't even be able to imagine or anticipate. They seem to come out of nowhere. I'm a really big networker. You have to be if you want to get outside your local community. I'm thinking of how things were back in the first couple of years of GYMGUYZ, and back then I did pretty much everything in the van—eat, talk on the phone, draw up schedules, and plan routes for the day. If I had to change clothes, I would do it in the back of the van. I got invited to a fancy event, a party where I had the chance to do some more networking. I shuffled some things around in my schedule so I could attend. It started at eight in the evening, and I had to look my best. I knew time was going to be tight, and I couldn't make time to go home for a shower. I finished my last session and put on my suit in the van. Everything was going great, until I ripped my pants hopping out of the van. I had options. I could have bought a new pair—but money was tight. I could drive home for a new pair, which would mean I would miss three-quarters of the party. Or I could subtly hold my pants a certain way so nobody would see the tear. I decided to go with option three. Luckily, the rip was in the back, so I could get away with it.

I did whatever I had to do in the beginning. When I was still working as a coach in addition to handling the entrepreneurial side of things, I was sleeping about three hours a night. I would start working at about three thirty in the morning and come home at midnight six days a week. One morning I was driving to a client at a quarter to four, and he was having work done on his house. I was so exhausted that I wasn't paying attention to what was going on around me. Walking up to the door, I stepped on a big glob of grease and tracked it through the entire house. I almost had a heart attack. They were going on vacation the next day. I had to get a cleaning company get in there and clean everything. Now all my coaches wear shoe covers in everyone's home.

Snow has proved to be a major obstacle on occasion. I remember one snowstorm we had that was a total whiteout—zero visibility. Some of my clients wanted to cancel, but I was so intent on keeping to the schedule that I insisted on showing up. It was a huge mistake. The roads were so bad that I couldn't even see the lanes. I had to get out of the van and clear off the road in front of me so I could see the lines and keep going straight—did I mention that I was wearing shorts at the time? I ended up being late, but I still got the sessions in.

Another time, I had a flat tire on the way to a client. This was the dead of winter. I got out, thinking that I'd carry the equipment to the client. Instead, I slipped on some ice and injured my elbow.

Then there are difficulties with being on the road itself. Franchising requires me to travel a lot. I stayed at some nice places and some nasty places. In one motel I seriously considered sleeping in the bathtub because the bed was so filthy. Did I say *one* motel? That's the opposite of an exaggeration. And the travel itself can be a pain. If you've got to fly, you're going to encounter delays. I've been on flights that were cancelled, some that were redirected to other states.

By reflecting on my initial scheduling struggles, I was able to learn a lot about how to budget—both time and money. I was losing time driving around, wasting money on gas. For five or six months, I was literally driving back and forth in different directions, fifteen miles one way to train a client, fifteen miles back the opposite direction for another client, and then back to the first direction. I did what I had to do, but I realized at the time that I could find a way to schedule things more efficiently. Some of these problems resolved themselves as GYMGUYZ grew. Being able to hire new coaches took the load off my back and of course made it easier to schedule sessions in multiple locations.

In fitness, there's a concept called plyometric training, which refers to exercises designed to reach maximum force production in minimal time. That's how I envisioned GYMGUYZ. Our business model strives for plyometric success. The coaching system and van setup are designed to franchise. The low overhead we started with didn't hurt either.

But there's risk to that strategy. Here's an example of a choice I made that a lot of entrepreneurs might think of as a mistake. I don't, precisely because it worked out well: I started GYMGUYZ in 2008, and we awarded our first franchise in 2014. That's an extremely fast time frame. I pulled the trigger on franchising without having the money. I said to myself, "I'll figure it out."

In business, you have to be able to take risks, and I've taken many. Franchising is one of the biggest risks you can take. People think franchising is nothing more than making money off your brand. What people don't see is that it's basically the same as starting another business, with all that a new business entails. It means more expenses, more people to train, and more mental effort. Now you've got twice as much to keep in your head.

I think it's worthwhile to lay out the basics of franchising to give you an idea of what's involved. The foundational concept is simple: a business (called the franchisor) provides access to their business model and trademarks to an interested party (the franchisee), who then uses the name, proprietary information, and model to provide the same service or product within a set geographical location. The franchisee will pay an initial start-up cost and annual fees, and they're granted a contract for a set amount of time. For a number of reasons, fast food restaurants have been extremely successful using this method.

Franchising goes back a long way, to the middle of the nineteenth century. The first companies to franchise ranged from sewing machines to soda pop. Not all of them were successful, simply because nothing ever is successful 100 percent of the time. Franchising is not quite like starting from scratch, but it's pretty close. Most businesses don't start turning a profit for at least three or four years. They almost inevitably lose money in the beginning.

GYMGUYZ was doing well for me; I was running a profitable business for myself, but the opportunity to start franchising—which had always been part of my vision—sort of dropped into my lap (actually, onto my plate of brownies, but we'll get to that in chapter 8), so I decided to take it. In my opinion, if you don't take risks, you're not going to maximize your reward. At that point, it was like I was starting over, and both companies were struggling. I had to use cash from the company that was making money to fund the new company. Franchising isn't easy. What it really comes down to is the vision and positivity. If you're not going to be positive, it's never going to work.

I knew I had to rely on my vision. If we were going to go worldwide, I wanted to be part of every step in that process. Remember that my vision involves improving the lives of all the people involved in the GYMGUYZ process: clients, coaches, franchisees, family members. I want people to love what they do for a living, and while I trusted my vision for making that possible, I felt more confident the more I was involved. So my franchising model comes with lots of oversight on my end. I take part in the hiring of coaches, training, marketing, and overall maintenance of each franchise. To that end, we have annual franchise conferences. We have training videos, webinars, phone calls, and everything you can think of. We set up a fund to assist with marketing. We help with social media. We hold five-day training seminars at our corporate headquarters in New York. We even come to visit your territory for two days to provide training on site.

We take such an active role in franchising because we understand how tough it is to succeed. And let's face it, we're not always the best judge of our own performance. You might have heard the saying, "Practice makes perfect." Well, I've also heard it countered with, "Practice makes permanent." You're not going to improve unless you learn as you go along. That takes persistence and attention. Keep doing what you're doing, and pay attention, both to your own activity and to what others in the same field do. Stay engaged in your business. Understand the problems and look for solutions. And don't be afraid to ask for help.

That's why I'm in constant contact with my GYMGUYZ family. That's why I'm always networking. Because we can all use a little help. I've sought mentors in my efforts to build a worldwide company, and it's always paid off for me. Now, I strive to be that mentor for others. I lead through education, but more importantly I lead by example.

If you take one idea from this chapter, make it this one: persistence beats smarts every time. That's what I mean when I say that every no gets you closer to a yes. You're going to hit a lot of bumps. Lot of rocky roads. Things might seem like they're falling apart every now and then. But if you're persistent, if you face the challenges and keep to your vision, you can overcome the obstacles. Embrace rejection, and use it as an opportunity to improve. Keep putting the wheels back on every time they fall off. It's not an easy ride, but you can get there.

7

WORK IS NOT A DIRTY WORD

One thing people don't like to talk about is how tough it is to be married and have a family. Marriage is not easy. To maintain a relationship at that level, you've got to learn to compromise. You've got to learn to understand someone else's motives, even when that person wants to keep them quiet (we're back to EI again). You've got to sacrifice. Parenting is equally as difficult, and probably more so. You can't reason with a toddler. Sacrifice becomes an even bigger part of your life. You need to cultivate patience as a parent, patience and an even temper. Even when being a parent is good and satisfying, it's still stressful. Above all, you've got to put in the effort to be part of a family. I don't care if your family consists of two members, twenty, or two thousand— it requires maintenance.

One reason people don't like to talk about these difficulties is because doing so can invite judgment. It's all about perception. You could appear to be a happy family like the Brady Bunch on the surface. Social media sites often compound the problem. People don't put up pictures of themselves feeling miserable. Just like you're going to clean up your house before you have company, you want to present the best version of yourself to the public. It's only in those moments of unguarded intimacy that we admit things are hard. It's almost as if we've turned work into a dirty word.

People don't judge the past; they judge the present. But the past is essential for understanding how the present came to be in its current form. That allows you to see that success is accompanied by failure. You have to experience failure too at times, but some people don't understand that. Michael Jordan missed shots in every game he ever played. That's life. You can't win everything. You might experience a perfect moment now and then, but nothing stays that way for very long.

That same concept translates to business. There's no such thing as a perfect marriage, no perfect job, no such thing as perfection. I know because I've tried. I've shopped to be perfect. I'm detail oriented, maybe even a little anal. Actually, very anal. I work hard to make things a certain way. I plan routes to make them efficient. I'm constantly on the lookout for better equipment, better training methods, and better ways of doing business. You paint your picture in the beginning, and then you've got to revisit it with a critical eye to see what could be improved.

It's very dark in the beginning, when you start a business. A lot of people don't understand that. It's extremely challenging. If people think success is going to happen right away, they've got it wrong. It's about patience, persistence, and being a painter, revising that picture. Painters, like everybody else, have to get the work done. Otherwise what's the point? There was a writer in the nineteenth century named Horatio Alger. His novels told the story of the American dream. His characters would start from nothing—often they were orphans—but with what he called "luck and pluck," they would become successful. Luck is pretty straightforward. In his stories, the characters would often cross paths with somebody rich who became a benefactor. Pluck, on the other hand, is how he referred to hard work. Sure, I've had some luck in my time, but none of it would have mattered if I hadn't been willing and able to work hard to capitalize on it.

Getting the work done requires discipline, and that applies to all aspects of life. I needed to save money so I could keep building GYMGUYZ, realizing the vision. One way to do that was to cut spending wherever I could, so I reduced my diet to the bare minimum. I stopped thinking of eating as something fun and made it purely practical. It was all about saving every penny to build the brand. I would eat tuna and peanut butter. In order to save a little money, all I would consume came in big containers I could get at Costco: all the tuna, bread, peanut butter, and jelly I could find. And I ate like that for as long as I could—almost two years. I'm nauseated by tuna now. I can't even be around it. But I no longer have to eat that way. I did what I needed to do when I needed to do it.

If you're disciplined, you learn to conserve your funds. Save money however you can. When I needed a printer, I didn't buy a new one; I asked around and found one that someone was getting rid of. I got every last drop of ink out of each printer cartridge. I held off renting office space as long as possible, and instead I worked out of my parents' dining room.

Discipline is also about going to work every day, whether it's easy or not. It's sometimes tempting to sleep in, especially if you're not feeling 100 percent. The problem then is that clients see you as unreliable. I kept going to work regardless of how I felt on any given day and regardless of what kind of day it was. I mentioned the trouble I had dealing with blizzards last chapter. Discipline got me out on the roads regardless of the weather.

I remember being out in another bad storm, with ice so bad that the van struggled to get traction on a hill. I got stuck and went sliding backward, and all I could think was that I'd be late to get to my client. When I finally got there, I realized that I had left equipment at the previous client's house, so it was back on the road. I didn't want to risk going back up that same hill, so I parked down at the bottom and ran up.

Another time I had twenty minutes to get to a client, and the van got a flat tire. So I left the van on the side of the road, grabbed a bag of equipment, and literally ran to the client's house in ninety-five-degree heat. I arrived at the client's house soaking wet with sweat. In my head as I was running, people were looking at me, and I was thinking they were wondering what the hell I was doing, with forty pounds on my back, sprinting down the road. It was probably a mile, and afterward I still had to get back to the van and arrange for it to be fixed. Can't stop won't stop, right?

I'll be the first to admit that I sometimes need a bit of urging to get my head out of work. When I tell you how hard I used to work, I mean I was practically killing myself. Some days I would do fifteen or sixteen hour-long sessions, starting at the crack of dawn. I used to have this client late at night, and he would frequently cancel. It was not a big deal once in a while, but he wouldn't respect my commitment enough to call me earlier in the day to let me know. I would get to his house and lug all the equipment from the van, and he'd come downstairs and say that he didn't have time or didn't feel like it. This guy was fit and strong. He was a big fan of heavy dumbbell presses. He wanted to work out in his basement, so I had to carry the dumbbells down the stairs. And that late in the day, I was at the point where my body felt like it was about to collapse. These days, we're very strict on our twenty-four-hour cancellation policy, but this was years ago and I was still building the business. I didn't want to lose clients over an issue like that, so I often didn't enforce the cancellation policy. Even so, this was my time, my effort. I understood that sometimes there's a challenge for the client, and I wouldn't charge for a session they had to miss at the last second.

Any number of difficulties can arise from that kind of relentless devotion to your work. For example, I'd get sick frequently because I was working so hard and not getting enough rest. I remember one morning I had to pull over in the van because I was going to throw up. I still had to get through the day. I used to throw my back out two or three times a month. The kinds of equipment we kept in the vans back then worked well, but it wasn't the easiest to handle. These days we have great, industrial pieces of equipment, but that's a product of advancing technology and my endless search for the best exercise aids. Back at the beginning, everything was bulky, heavy, and awkward to carry. I couldn't let that stop me, though. I was developing the blueprint, figuring it out for when I was ready to hire other people. I've tried out a wide spectrum of exercise gear to see what works best—equipment on wheels, in bags, disassembled ... I had to find the best of every piece. I suffered because of that. But I don't count it as a mistake. The only way to find out was to test everything we thought might work for us. So much of life is trial and error.

And just because you're established doesn't mean the need for discipline and hard work will end. I've been working like an animal for the last couple of months to complete the process of franchising into Canada. It's a lot more work than it was to start in the United States. I've got to Canadianize everything. There are trademark differences, agreements, an entirely different currency rate and legal system. Even though I anticipated differences—remember:

going worldwide was part of the initial vision—it's still a massive amount of time and energy.

Franchising in the United States is still a big part of my daily work. There's the conference to organize. There are franchise visits and training seminars. And there's the process of choosing which applicants receive them. Remember, GYMGUYZ is a family, so vetting our new members is a lengthy process that we take seriously.

On top of that, the fitness world is always changing. People are developing new methods and new equipment all the time. If you want to succeed in the fitness world, you've got to keep up with all of the new techniques and developments. That alone is hard work.

The concept of hard work applies equally well to training and fitness. I know that's obvious, but it's worth saying out loud. One reason people often take on partners when they become entrepreneurs is that a second person can help motivate you to keep working when it's easy to slack off. The same holds true for exercise. That's why I like to say that the GYMGUYZ job is never done. Yes, it's to our advantage to keep clients long-term, but our clients get just as much out of our sessions as we do. There's nothing like having someone there to provide motivation, to lay out exactly what you need to do to meet your goals. That's why exercise classes can be effective and why people work out in groups. With people expecting you to show up, you're more likely to do the work.

Remember, my vision is about making life better for people. GYMGUYZ does that job by making it easier for you to meet your training goals. We come to you, so you don't have to worry about how you look in a public place. I know that's why some people avoid the gym—they don't want to deal with other people around them. For some people, those other people are a motivation. For others, they're an obstacle. We've got all kinds of clients.

I hope that my struggles along the way, detailed in this and the previous chapter, show you that hard work pays off. Seeing that example of hard work is more important that we typically think it is. The grind is necessary, even though it's not glamorous. Movies and TV shows like to tell stories about the eureka moment, when a detective or scientist or artist sees the light and solves an impossible problem. That's exciting, that's dramatic. The problem is—it's not how life usually works. Isaac Newton wouldn't have figured out gravity just by sitting under an apple tree. He had spent a lifetime studying how the world works. Einstein wasn't really a failing student. He spent every day working out math equations, studying hard and pushing himself to learn more. No professional athlete gets by on raw talent. You've got to work hard to refine your talents into skills and apply them to situations as they arise. If you look at talent levels between amateur and professional sports, you can see a huge gap. Once you begin to do something full time, you see how well discipline pays off.

The good news is, it doesn't matter where you start. You can begin with nothing more than a desire. As long as you paint that picture and are willing to find the discipline necessary to get the job done, you can make it happen. You've got to keep at it every day. Work is not a dirty word.

FUEL

One thing I love about being an entrepreneur is the process of building something from nothing. Sure, there are lots of other ways to go about that same thing, but none of them combine the specific resources I had available to me with my goals and talents the way entrepreneurship does. I'm sure if I hadn't hit onto the idea of providing mobile exercise—"You name the place ... we bring the gym," as our initial slogan read—something else would have come along, some other idea or opportunity. But I hit the nail on the head with GYMGUYZ.

At first it was just me, driving the van all over town, making appointments and working as the coach. I knew that to make that vision real, I would need to surround myself with great people— people who could see the vision with me, who were both willing to take a risk and able to help GYMGUYZ take its place on the worldwide stage.

Not everyone is willing, of course (remember the coach who left us high and dry from chapter 4? I'm still grateful to my brother Jason for stepping in when I needed it), and not everyone who is willing is capable. Sometimes someone just isn't right for the family. That's maybe the toughest thing about my position, but it's a reality that every entrepreneur is going to have to face. I can only hope that those people with whom we've had to part ways will understand that, truly and honestly, it was never personal.

I bring this up because, though family is the most vital component of GYMGUYZ, it's not the only one. I view this enterprise through the lens of FUEL. I want to spell it out: fun, unity, earnings, and leadership. That last one is important. Yes, we're a family, and yes, we are united in the endeavor of earning and having fun, but a leader sometimes has to make hard decisions, such as letting people go or turning down a potential franchisee. Being a leader means recognizing when something isn't working. And when a member of the family is holding everyone back, isn't capable of taking us to the next level, something has to change. It kills me to do it, but it has to be done.

Let's take a look at the rest of FUEL. This might be obvious, but it's worth pointing out that fuel is what makes motion possible. It allows you freedom to move and improve. Without it, you're stuck. The car won't run.

Fun. Remember when you were a kid, and instead of walking, you ran, jumped, hopped, and tumbled everywhere you went. Running was fun. More than fun, it was the only way to move.

You didn't exercise, you relished the fact that your body was in motion. That's how we want everyone to feel when they work out. That's where the coaches come in. They're so important because they make the experience into something more than exercise— they show our clients what's possible. And on top of that list of possibilities is fun. Fun transforms exercise from a grueling obligation into something to look forward to. This is especially important because as a coach you're going to encounter clients who maybe would rather not be there. Sometimes parents sign up their kids, who don't have a say in it. You've got to win them over. That's why you've got to always be positive.

I also want everyone within the GYMGUYZ family to have fun with each other, so we organize volleyball and laser tag games. At our corporate office, we go out to eat together, watch movies together, and put on other events designed to make everyone feel like a vital part of this family. By having fun together, we work toward the second element of FUEL: unity.

Unity. It means everyone in the GYMGUYZ family is on the same page. To foster unity, we get to know each other. So we have an annual conference where our franchise family members can share experiences and ideas. I make my family members' well-being my priority. I know them by name. We talk regularly. There's a tendency for CEOs to distance themselves from others within the same organization, but that's not how I operate. If we were going to work as a unit, I knew that I had to be there with everybody else. You've probably heard the phrase, "Teamwork makes the dream work." We live by that saying. Without teamwork, it won't work. Unity makes scalability possible.

Earnings. Chase the vision, and the money will follow. If you're only after the money, you might get it, but you also run a great risk. If you are only becoming an entrepreneur to get rich, what happens if you fail? (Yes, I said that you shouldn't build failure into your business model, but bear with me.) If you chase the money and fail in the process, you've got nothing. But if you're in it for something other than money, if you're in it to help others improve their lives … if it all falls apart, you'll have at least done that much good. If the enterprise itself is worth the while, you'll never truly fail.

I've got to be honest here: I was paying people six-figure salaries before I took home anything close to that. I learned early on that it's important to be happy doing great things for my family. I recognized that it's important not only for my mental well-being, but also for the family as a whole. Teamwork makes the dream work. Improving the lives of those around me was just as important—and sometimes more important—as my own. It has paid off.

That brings us back to **leadership**. My role in GYMGUYZ is to figure out where we're going and how we're going to get there: to make the vision a reality. To do that, I don't think about tomorrow; I think about several years from now. That's why it's so important to surround myself with talented people. I put my trust in them to handle the day-to-day on most occasions: working *in* the business. That way, I can focus on taking us to the next level: working *on* the business.

I need to devote my time and energy to scaling. Things are constantly changing, so I've got to come up with new ways to engage so we can keep up with those changes. People ask me how we have grown so fast, franchising in just a few years. The answer's simple: FUEL. Without it, we're stagnant. With it, we're unstoppable. We achieve scalability.

Scalability is a business model's capacity for growth. If a company can retain its performance, efficiency, and profit as it expands, it's considered scalable. In other words, to what extent can a model accommodate an increase in size? Will it work on different scales—small, medium, large? Or to stick with the idea of having a vision: can the eight-by-ten image be blown up to eight hundred by one hundred? Is it going to lose some clarity and get fuzzy if it's put on a gigantic canvas? Scale is a powerful thing, but you have to know how to do it. I wasn't taught; it's intuition. It's the idea that what you do with five people can be done—in terms of similar levels of efficiency or productivity—with five thousand people. When it's put that way, I hope you can see what an awesome concept scalability is. It's the only way to make the vision of worldwide a reality.

Of course, that doesn't mean growth is easy. Some ideas just don't scale well. But let me tell you, GYMGUYZ was scalable from the beginning.

Scaling requires attention to detail. When considering growth, you've got to consider every aspect of your business model and what effect an increase will have on your ability to provide your goods or services. GYMGUYZ was never about selling people products. We want to improve the lives of our clients, and understanding that element is vital to scalability. That means personal attention. When I started out, I had to do everything, which meant a lot of time on the phone, a lot of time assessing our clients to figure out the right regimen for them, and a lot of time on the road, getting to and from appointments.

Looking back, it's hard to believe how rudimentary my methods were at the beginning. Clients would often want to pay up front for a certain number of training sessions, so I'd write down how many they had paid for on index cards. That meant I literally had to take a pen and cross off each session they did so I could keep track of how many sessions they had coming. Talk about an idea without scalability. I mean, sure, you could do it for thousands of clients, but it's so much easier to set it all up with computer software. And even then, it was a week's worth of work just to transfer of all the information from the index cards into the program. That was a tough week.

Luckily, I had already brought in some other family members by that point. Early on, about 2012, when I was still working out of my parents' dining room, I was also adding coaches to the family. I didn't want to interview prospective coaches at the dinner table, obviously, but I didn't have a lot of alternatives. I decided to meet people in coffee shops, worried still about how sincerely I'd be taken in that setting. But even in situations like that, you have to do the best you can.

One of the women who was applying to be a coach impressed me right away. She had a background in training but was also an accountant, a CPA. I was impressed by her resume and could see that she was talented. I saw that she was extremely talented, a very smart, level-headed individual with a lot of drive. As you know, drive is what I'm all about, so I thought she would be a great addition to our team. The first time we met, I pulled out the brush and started painting my vision to show her where we were going. She believed in it. Two months later, we got our first office.

Getting that office space was a big decision, and it kept me up some nights. Suddenly, I had to pay rent. On top of that, I wanted to add more vans to our fleet. Keep in mind that we stock each van with three hundred sixty-five pieces of equipment. New family members, new location, new details to attend to. I was worried, yeah, but not a lot. After two weeks of starting the business, I understood that I was really on to something. The demand was insane. And it only kept growing.

So we'd found ourselves a small office space. We made the most of it. We had one wall painted bright red because that's our color. Red is motivating. It represents power, strength, passion, determination, and desire. It's energizing, and it excites the emotions. It motivates us to take action. I wanted everyone who walked in to see that, to know that we sweat red.

The place was cramped. I had to share a desk with our office manager (it helped that I was out working as a coach a lot during this time). We had one phone, and we didn't even have call waiting. But with our office in good hands, I was able to focus on scaling and growing. I didn't have to worry about the books anymore. Still, it was tough. Growth always is: we have growing pains in our bodies, after all. In an entrepreneurial environment, those growing pains can take the form of worries, such as when it was time for me to cut back on the amount of training and assessments I did. That was something I struggled with, but it was a natural part of the growth of GYMGUYZ. Handing over the phones and the assessments was necessary because it was time for me to work on the business instead of in the business. Because I planned to take GYMGUYZ worldwide, I had to trust my family.

It paid off. I brought on another family member. She had been running a business for a while and was looking for another opportunity. You've got to be able to see talent. I attached this new family member to my hip and taught her everything I knew. Soon enough, she ended up taking over new appointments. That way, I could focus on franchising.

We kept adding coaches and vans, and before too long, we needed more space for our office. We'd been scaling vertically for a few years, and now it was time to scale horizontally.

At that point, I had to figure out how franchising was going to work. This really got me fired up. I believed in the vision, but that didn't mean I had every step planned out. I had to start thinking of all the details. How big would the basic territory for each franchise be? What kinds of support would we provide? How would we train our franchise family members? How much would it cost? That's on top of the standard elements of franchising, such as permits and licensing, certifications, franchising fees, insurance, and the list goes on. Franchising isn't something to approach lightly. In fact, sometimes it seemed impossible. Impossible is a negative word, so slice it down the center. You've got to stay positive.

How we sold our first franchise is pretty awesome. It starts with my wife, Stacy, being pregnant with our son. At that point, I hadn't taken a vacation since I started the business. It had been about six years. You've probably heard about couples taking a trip before having a baby, trying to relax before it finally happens. We thought, with the holidays coming up and the baby on the way, it would be a good idea to take a break. We decided to take a vacation in Cabo San Lucas.

I was so nervous to go away because it was the first time I'd left the business completely in the hands of my family members. Remember, I had a hard time letting someone else do the assessments, and now I was about to leave the country, putting full faith in them. So I struggled at first, but by the time I got there, I was in heaven. I remember getting out of the cab at the hotel when we first arrived. Everything was open and gorgeous. You could see the ocean. Stacy wanted me to fully relax, so she told me to leave my phone in the room whenever we went out. She said nothing was going to change in a couple of hours, so I should take it easy. I did my best …

To understand how it all played out, you need to know that I love brownies. No, I really love brownies. You can imagine that I keep tight control over what I eat most of the time (more on that later, in chapter 10), so when I'm not following my regular routine, I take the opportunity to indulge. The second night in Cabo, I got on a buffet line and filled a plate full of brownies. I stacked them up, at least fifteen of them.

This guy came over to me and said, "Who's that for?"

"Me," I said.

He couldn't believe it. "You're eating all those, and you look like that?"

"Absolutely," I said. "I'm on vacation."

Well, he loved it. We start talking, and eventually the conversation turned to the usual. What do you do for a living, that sort of thing. I told him about GYMGUYZ, and he got really interested. He said that his son would love to hear about it. Next thing you know, I was FaceTiming with his son. Two weeks later, we came back from Cabo and closed the deal.

I pitched that story to *Entrepreneur Magazine*, which devoted a full-page article to it in 2014. Before too long, the *New York Times* did an article on us. We've been featured in the *Wall Street Journal*, on CNBC, and on nearly every major news network. These opportunities created more and more exposure. Once you get on stage, it becomes easier and easier to stay there. But it's hard to break in, which is why I took advantage of every opportunity to get our name out there and why I created some of my own. Recently, we were ranked one of the fastest-growing franchises in 2017. We even got into *People* magazine. Wow, we're really doing it. We're making it happen. Everything I say will come true, because we're going to make it happen. We do not stop. As I write this, GYMGUYZ is still growing. Within five years, we'll have hundreds and hundreds of franchises, and we're now international.

The vision is becoming reality. Behind those numbers and feature articles is the fact that lives are changing for the better. I've seen it firsthand among our family members, grinding it out every day in the office and conducting training sessions. They're happy to work in an environment they love. And I see it among our franchise family members. From them, I've learned how much love you can create in this world. It can be tough sometimes; business is hard, just like anything that's worthwhile. But because you're family, you're still going to love each other at the end of the day.

As the vision started to become reality, we were able to do something that demonstrates in no uncertain terms how valuable our contribution can be. We started putting testimonials up on the company website. With technology that wasn't even imagined half a century ago, we're able to let people tell their own stories, in their own words, about how GYMGUYZ has helped them live the lives they've only been able to imagine. You can watch videos in which they share the success they've experienced with our coaches. You can hear our franchise family members talk about how they've found satisfaction in their careers.

That's the real payoff. I've always wanted to change people's lives, help them achieve their goals, on both the client and the entrepreneurial sides. A lot of people want to go into business but can't because they need that structure, they need a blueprint, an established infrastructure, and by making GYMGUYZ into a franchise, I've set it up for them. I've worked for years to set up that structure.

Seeing people smile, reading the emails that I've gotten, these are the goals that I set out to achieve as an entrepreneur. Some people never have the guts to do what I've done, to take the risks. So when I get an email from a franchise family member that says joining the GYMGUYZ family is the best decision they've ever made, that GYMGUYZ has changed not only their life but the lives of their family … That's the payoff.

DRIVE

Individually, we all have limits. Together, nothing is impossible.

I can't tell you how many times I've heard people lamenting things they wish they'd done, places they'd gone, risks they'd taken. It's sad to see wasted potential, unfulfilled dreams, and regrets. I make sure those things can never be said about me. I drive hard, and I always get where I'm going.

Some people don't. They start down one road only to turn off and go in another direction. It's easy to get distracted. To overcome this challenge, you've got to focus. You've got to feel driven to make the vision a reality.

You might have noticed that I'm into acronyms, abbreviations, and mottos. FUEL. The Three Cs. "Teamwork Makes the Dream Work". DRIVE is just as important: Determination, Respect, Integrity, Versatility, and Excellence. I've laid the groundwork for these concepts throughout the entire book, so now it's time to dig into the specifics.

Determination. When a budding entrepreneur asks for my help and doesn't follow through, it's probably because of a lack of determination. Maybe they misplaced my contact information. Maybe they forgot about it. Maybe they got caught up in another project. The reason for not following through doesn't matter. Determination matters. Determination is important because it separates the people with regrets from those who succeed. It's a willingness to do what needs to be done to make the vision into reality. It's about willpower and the ability to focus. It's the capacity to set your jaw, clench your fists, and get the job done no matter what.

This is such an important part of life that we make movies about it, like *Rocky*. These movies inspire us to the extent that Rocky, a fictional character, even has a statue devoted to him on the steps of the Philadelphia Art Museum. It's one of the most famous tourist attractions in the city.

Sometimes, determination is all it takes to make things happen, but in a lot of cases, determination needs to be accompanied by quick thinking, resourcefulness, and planning. Yet without determination behind it, an enterprise begun by someone with all those traits will most likely flounder. All the resources in the world won't guarantee success if you lack the determination to put them to their best use. That's why DRIVE starts with determination.

Respect. To me, the most important part of the word *respect* is that little prefix *re* at the beginning. Redo, repeat, rehash, replicate. Do it again. It means that you're prepared to do something the same way more than once, and that's key. You need to be able to look back on the things you do and still feel good about them. This applies foremost to how you treat other people, and it applies to yourself. We're in Golden Rule territory here.

Do unto others … But I also think it's important to consider the flip side: don't do to other people what you wouldn't want done to you. This is especially important when you're in the business of providing a service to your clients.

Respect is about putting yourself in someone else's shoes, thinking about how you'd react in their situation. If you respect someone, you're not going to leave a job halfway complete. You're going to give it everything you've got. That's what we do at GYMGUYZ. We embody respect in our hiring, our franchising, and our service.

But let's not forget that it's important to respect yourself. It all starts with you, after all. In some ways, building a business from nothing is impossible without self-respect.

Integrity. I almost hate to say it, that whole "being true to yourself" deal, but it's worth thinking about. Because that's what integrity is, and if you're going against your better judgment, it's going to affect your integrity. Integrity means that you're integrated, that all your parts are working together. The gears are in motion, and their teeth all line up. It means that you can't see the seams—the face is on the watch, so the cogs are hidden. Everything is complete.

You need to demonstrate integrity in everything you do. For GYMGUYZ, it's a simple concept: we're sincere and uncompromising in our drive to do the right thing. If you see someone drop a dollar, pick it up and give it back to them. You have to have that same mentality in your business, across the board. If you don't, things aren't going to work out in your favor. It all ties back into our business model. Our coaches are going to lead you through the best exercise routines you'll ever experience. When we talk about integrity, what we're really talking about is being a genuine person.

I was in a customer's home while he was getting work done on the house, and a worker stole a watch. I wasn't sure if it was the worker's watch or it was the homeowner's, but it looked like it was the homeowner's. You don't want to accuse someone of a crime, but when you talk about honesty and integrity, you have to be willing to put it into practice. So I reported what I'd seen, and the customer got the watch back. In short, you need to be a good person, because honesty and being a good person will always come back to be a win for you.

That's why we do extensive assessments for each client. That's why I conduct interviews the way I do. Each new addition to GYMGUYZ, clients, coaches, franchisees, and the rest, is a gear in the machine. And you've got to make sure it's not only the right size and shape but that you know exactly how it fits. Each piece has a job to do, and sometimes more than one.

Versatility. We're always going to face challenges, so we have to evolve. If you don't evolve as a brand, you're not going to grow. In tech, customer service … how we engage in these domains is constantly changing, so you've got to be able to change with it.

In chapter 5, discussing execution, I brought up the idea that to succeed you need to be able to be friends with both a millionaire and a criminal. That's versatility in action. Remember that you've got to be able to be friends with both categories of people, not just interact with them in a superficial way. This doesn't mean pandering or being disingenuous; don't forget respect and integrity. Friendship is deeper, rooted in commonality and compatibility. That means seeing the good side of others, seeing something in everyone that's worth your time and effort.

I'm big on observation, seeing as much as possible in every situation. And I think that you've got to be able to process what you observe. Think things through—think *everything* through.

This is, of course, exactly what a painter does. Compositions don't happen by accident. The painter sketches out rough drafts—thumbnails—and has to be willing to go over them again and again to get it right.

Notice that a lot of good painters, in fact, the best painters, are also versatile. Michelangelo was a sculptor, Da Vinci was an engineer, Picasso … Picasso would take just about anything and turn it into art. He looked at a bicycle seat and handlebars and saw the head of a bull. I'm not saying you need to be a Renaissance man to succeed as an entrepreneur, but why not go for it? Why not branch out? When you're painting your vision, use all resources you have, and then find new ones.

The early days of GYMGUYZ were tough in part because we had to wear a lot of hats. Answering phones, coaching clients, advertising and marketing, handling the books: I had to do it all. Even when I was able to bring in talented people to help, everyone still had to do multiple jobs to make the business run as smoothly as possible. Now we're able to specialize more, but those early experiences were invaluable. It's a learning process, and the more you know about what's going on at all levels, the better leader you can be.

Many of the greatest minds in history show us the value of versatility. Study the best to become the best.

Excellence. Nothing's perfect, so I always keep in mind the number 85 percent. That's a solid B in school, and that's not bad. To really understand excellence, look at professional sports. I'm a lifelong New York Islanders fan, so let's take them as an example. In the 2016–2017 season, the player who scored the most goals was Anders Lee (note that this isn't the highest total points), with thirty-four. That's 34 goals out of 191 shots, for a percentage of

17.8. Looking at baseball, the leading hitters are successful only about three times in ten.

The point here is that when you're at the top, nobody expects 100 percent. Perfection simply is not realistic, not on an everyday basis. One hundred percent every day isn't sustainable, especially not by an individual. But like athletic teams, you need to have excellent people around you who can take up the slack and push your family to the next level.

Keep that DRIVE mentality.

I've gone into detail here because I've heard advice that sounds like it's the opposite. You've probably heard someone say, "Fake it till you make it." Now, I agree and disagree with that piece of advice. On the one hand, projecting confidence when you don't really feel it can work in your benefit. But on the other hand, at the end of the day, some stuff just can't be faked. I want to rephrase it: Focus till you make it. Focus drives your business, allows you to scale, and becomes the stepping stone to get you to the next level.

A lot of employers say they want people who are good at multitasking. The philosophy behind this is that doing more than one thing at a time increased productivity. I tend to disagree. Do one job at a time, and put all your energy into the job in front of you. Sure, there are exceptions. Some tasks don't require 100 percent focus. The problem is, it's easy to develop bad habits. The one exception that I do like is combining physical and mental exertion. By engaging in an activity that you can do on autopilot, your mind can actually do some of its best work.

The components of DRIVE are, importantly, widely achievable. I don't want you to get the idea that I'm the only one who can do this. I think everyone's the same when it comes down to it. Notice that a lot of the parts of DRIVE come in the form of effort and willpower: integrity, determination, respect—these are traits that don't require a particular set of skills. They require you to be mentally tough, sure, but you don't have to practice for hours every day to achieve them. Versatility and excellence are harder to achieve, but they also don't require you to be a genius or virtuoso. Those talents will help, of course, but they won't get the job done. To succeed, you need to have more than just an idea. You need to turn dreams into goals.

A dream is kind of vague, blurred around the edges. It lacks the clarity that you see in real life. A dream is nothing more than a seed. It needs cultivation and care to sprout, and even then, the job isn't done. You've got to water it, keep the soil full of nutrients. For a dream, the same process means systematically thinking through what you need to do to make it come true. That means being realistic about what's possible and then figuring out how to do the impossible.

Look at it this way: entrepreneurship is living a couple of years of your life like most people won't so you can live the rest of your life like most people can't. That's one of those sayings that gets thrown around a lot, but it does apply. Business is not for everyone. It requires sacrifice, risk, and mental endurance. I ate a lot of garbage from other people for years as they belittled me because they didn't believe in the vision. I've already told you how I sacrificed, eating tuna and peanut butter for years so I could put everything I made back into the business. I was willing to play the long game.

The long game requires patience; without the ability to stay calm as you wait for things to play out, for your planning and vision to pay off, your business will never work. You can't just keep altering everything. You've got to trust your plans, your instincts, and your family.

Now, there are two kinds of patience, and both are important. The first is probably what comes to mind when someone says the word: waiting, maybe in a doctor's office, for something to happen. Back to hockey: you've got on your gear, stick in hand, and are waiting for the ref to drop the puck. There's literally nothing you can do until that happens.

The second kind is the patience required to do something that takes a long time. It's the patience required to master a skill, to see the results of daily exercise, to complete a puzzle, or to memorize all the bones in the body. It's an active patience, and as a result, it requires you to maintain focus.

Being an entrepreneur requires both of these kinds of patience. You're going to have to wait once you've filed paperwork, with nothing to do until it's processed. And you're going to have to be patient as you start your business, pounding the pavement to get the word out, drumming up clients and setting things into motion. Results take time.

During that time, the world is going to take a lot of shots at you, and you won't always see them coming. Some will hit and some will miss, so you have to be prepared. In order to get to the top of the mountain, you've got to crawl, bite, scratch, kick, do whatever you have to do to get to the top.

Being an entrepreneur can be a lot like being on a roller coaster. You've got to be strapped in tight. You're going to feel a sense of dread as it starts, when you hear the click of the cars as they ascend that first hill. You might even feel a little helpless. It will seem like it takes forever to get to the top, but once you're there, it's a thrill. Once you're there, you can hardly focus on anything else.

And focus is important because as you build your business, you're going to have to deal with other people's perceptions. You craft an image, the one you want, but you can't always control how other people perceive what's going on. People will perceive your business differently than you do; there's no way around that. You can understand this by looking into other companies, especially on their websites. They put their best face forward, and so you won't often see any negative reviews. But no one really knows the guts of a business except for the people running it. They're not going to tell you they're losing money. Who's going to be honest and tell you they're doing horribly?

Remember too that a roller coaster is driven by many mechanisms—pulleys, engines, and above all, gravity. In that sense, you'd think they're out of control, until you remember that they're on a track. That's the vision, the painting, the work you put into your enterprise long before you put the wheels onto the track. It's the long game, and you've got to have patience to win it.

BALANCE

I already told you about how GYMGUYZ opened its first franchise. Things came together in a way that I never would have expected, and if you want to become an entrepreneur, don't rely on that kind of luck. Instead, you've got to cultivate discipline and fall in love with patience.

Discipline is vital to success. It's important to think of discipline in two ways. First, you've got to be able to get started and do the job that needs to be done. We touched on determination in the previous chapter, and that applies here as well. Discipline involves focus. It means not allowing yourself to be distracted by the thousands of other things trying to steal your attention.

But there's another side to discipline that doesn't get a lot of attention. If the first side is being able to get started and sticking with the job; the flip side is the ability to stop yourself when necessary. Most tasks can't be done all at once, and it can be a mistake to try to finish in one manic moment. This applies to exercise—if you push yourself too hard, especially at the beginning, you're going to get hurt. So the trick is to decide what your workout will be for the day and then stick to it, no matter if you feel like you could run an extra few miles or do another ten reps. It also applies to anything you want to do, any way you want to improve yourself. Studying too hard makes all the information nothing more than a jumble. Sleep helps your brain to process all the information you took in during the day. It's necessary. Discipline is the ability to tell yourself that you've got to take a break.

Both elements of discipline can be easier to enforce if you develop a routine. Over the years, I've developed one that works for me. Here's how my basic weekday goes.

I get up between three and three thirty in the morning. I jump in the shower right away, and then have breakfast. I eat the same thing every day: oatmeal with a tablespoon of peanut butter, and a protein shake. That doesn't change, because it works.

Then I head to the gym for a workout. When I used to work as a coach, the workout would be easy because I could just open up the doors to the van and exercise. Nowadays I work out in a gym. I use weights every day, but I vary the cardio a lot, sometimes boxing, running sprints, things like that to keep it interesting.

Some people work out hard for a while, then they ease back and just maintain what they've achieved. Not me. Just like in business, where you always want to be smarter than you were yesterday, every day I want my body to be better than it was the day before. My workout takes from forty-five to ninety minutes, and the whole time I'm pushing myself as hard as I can each day. It's the ultimate satisfaction.

Exercise must be balanced. Take time to let your mind and body rest. You've got to think about how your workout is going to affect you over a long period of time. I work out five days a week, resting for two days in between. Every twelve weeks, I take a week off. Giving your body that kind of rest allows you to recover. Exercise strains your body, so you've got to give it time to heal all the little tears and bruises that accumulate from pushing it hard. You also need to rest to let your nervous system recover. I try to coordinate these exercise breaks with times when I have to travel, but it doesn't always line up nicely. When I travel and still have to work out, I usually avoid the gyms in the hotels because they're not up to my standards. I'll travel an hour to find a good hardcore gym if I have to.

That's one value of your routine: your body gets used to doing something at the same time every day, so it gets ready for activity. It's important to keep to that routine, because if you skip a day, you'll notice the differences in your body. You might not have as much energy. You might not feel quite right for the rest of the day. Your body remembers.

Some of my best ideas come to me when I'm working out, and they develop as I'm cooling off afterward. My brain is always working. Sometimes I'll wake up in the middle of the night with an idea, so I grab my phone and get to work on it. I've actually considered trying to find a waterproof pad of paper so I can jot down notes when I'm showering, instead of having to stop in the middle to write something down.

Then I finish getting ready for work, and in what I wear, I want to communicate who I am. Let me break that down for you. I wear shorts to work every single day, whether it's ten degrees or one hundred. It doesn't matter. That's me. Of course I dress up when I have important meetings, when someone's coming in who's interested in a franchise. But on a normal day, I dress how I'm comfortable.

Finally, I'm ready to hit the office, I'm consistent. I bring a cup of blueberries and two and a half liters of water every day, and I try to get to the office between six thirty and seven thirty.

All this preparation, it's really about separating yourself from the rest of the pack. Distinguish yourself through willpower, endurance, creativity, and focus. To be extraordinary, you can't live ordinary. I was always different. I feel like I've achieved a lot already in my career, and I've been able to do so partly because I operate with the mentality that someone is trying to take it from me. I work hard to make sure that won't happen. I never quit. I had hernia surgery and was told to stay home for a week, but I was back at work the next day. I cannot be stopped. That's what it all comes down to.

The way I maintain this kind of schedule is straightforward. I eat very clean, at least during the workweek. My diet consists of things like grilled chicken, steak, vegetables, carbs (rice or potatoes), good stuff. Protein for the muscles, carbs for the energy.

Every day, work is a little different. There are conferences to organize, new equipment to test and explore, expenses to review, meetings to hold … It never ends. I try to get home between five and seven. Sure, some days I'm at work until eight or nine o'clock. But even then, I try to meet up with my wife and son at the park and then take my son for pizza and ice cream. Every night I make sure to give my son a bath and put him to bed. That gives me time with my wife.

I get to bed between eleven and midnight. I'm trying to work out a way to get more sleep, but it's challenging because my brain is always working. And again, discipline is important.

As valuable as a routine is, it's also important to break from it. People do this in a lot of different ways. You can't always think about work. People like to talk about balancing work and home life, but in my experience, it's more about separation. You have to know when to shut it off. So on Sundays I sleep in a little, until four. Then I play hockey until seven thirty.

If you're looking to relieve some stress through physical activity, it doesn't get better than hockey. I've been playing since I was about six years old, and it only gets more fun with time. I usually play left wing or center. There's nothing better than turning it up, skating past two defensemen while showing off a nice stick handling move, and scoring a goal. That's my getaway. I mean getaway in a physical sense but also in a mental sense. When I'm exercising, my brain is working just as hard as my body—in fact the physical activity can help your brain think. But hockey's different. The only time I *don't* think is when I'm playing hockey, when I'm on the ice. It's all action. It's good to take your head off your body and put it in a box for a while.

I like hockey for a lot of reasons, but one of them is the teamwork involved. Hockey's almost never a one-man show. Even when there's a star leading a team, remember that it took an entire professional organization to put that one player on the ice. An offense is nothing without good defense, and good defense can't win a game if your team doesn't score any goals.

Weekends are also time to loosen up a bit on diet. I love pizza and brownies. Those are my two favorite things, so I will indulge every now and then. Sometimes I'll pick up fifteen doughnuts and eat them all in one sitting. Not the best thing for me, maybe, but so far, so good.

I try to maintain a wall between work and home, but I do spend some time on my phone and occasionally stop by the office on Sundays. It would be a lot harder without my wife. Stacy has proved to be everything I could want in my life. I'm not always easy to get along with. I've got a lot of crazy ways. In the career of any entrepreneur, there is always a special person behind the scenes. She's not necessarily the one helping me make business decisions, but she understands. She's a rock-solid support. She's always there for me when I need it. When I'm overwhelmed with stress and need some guidance, I can count on her. At the end of the day, we all need someone like that.

Stacy and I are different in a lot of ways. If you can't tell, I'm an intense guy. I talk fast, and I'm always on the move. I get up at three in the morning, even when I've got nothing to do. Stacy, she goes with the flow. She's easygoing, which is one of the big reasons we work as a couple. She says she likes to live in the moment. I'm a planner—remember the vision? That's a method of planning.

So how does our relationship work? It's not as hard as it seems. We connect where it counts. One way I knew that we would work was because we talked for a week on the phone before even seeing a picture of each other. We had a friend in common who thought we should meet, this was in the early days of GYMGUYZ, before we had our first franchise. Our schedules never overlapped, so there wasn't a chance of us meeting. But this friend knew us both, and she thought we would get along. We started talking on the phone, and after about a week, we thought it was a good idea to meet in person. In other words, we got to know each other's personality.

Marriage is work, just like everything else that's worthwhile. Even though we're different sorts of people, we know how to have fun together. All the other stuff, like paying bills, maintaining a home, choosing how to raise our son—which can be very, very hard, even in the easiest relationship—goes a lot more smoothly if you can have fun together. Stacy and I both think of fun in terms of doing things together. We stay active, whether it's going to the adventure park to ride the rides or just being outside together. You've got to get out there and experience life. Get the most out of every day.

On top of all that, Stacy encourages me to keep my work and home lives separate. We try to have date nights here and there. And she'll say, "Why don't you just take a day?" every now and then. This is even more important now that we're parents. Vacations with a child are a whole different challenge. I'm not laying out at the pool; I have to keep my eyes on my child. I do plan to take a vacation soon, but for right now, I'm tied to both my families.

In that way, being a parent is a whole lot like being an entrepreneur. Remember the old saying: An entrepreneur is willing to live like most people won't for a short time in order to live like most people can't. To succeed in both parenting and running a business, you've got to play the long game. It takes time—it doesn't happen in a year or two years. Put in the time. Outwork everyone else. Think on your feet. Be patient, and let the hard times pass. If you're not patient enough to let your plans unfold and scale, you're not going to succeed. Meet the challenges head-on, and climb that mountain to get to the promised land on the other side. Envision yourself there. I can already see myself walking into my next office building when we outgrow our current space. The image is so clear in my mind. I can practically paint it with my eyes shut. Fall in love, with an enterprise, with other people, with patience. It will pay off.

Printed in the United States
By Bookmasters